D1563634

POLITICAL PHILOSOPHY AS THERAPY

Contributions in Political Science
Series Editor: Bernard K. Johnpoll

American Democratic Theory: Pluralism and Its Critics
William Alton Kelso

International Terrorism in the Contemporary World
Marius H. Livingston, with Lee Bruce Kress and Marie G. Wanek, editors

Doves and Diplomats: Foreign Offices and Peace Movements in Europe and America in the Twentieth Century
Solomon Wank, editor

Believing Skeptics: American Political Intellectuals, 1945-1964
Robert Booth Fowler

Locke, Rousseau, and the Idea of Consent: An Inquiry into the Liberal Democratic Theory of Political Obligation
Jules Steinberg

Judicial Craftsmanship or Fiat?: Direct Overturn by the United States Supreme Court
Howard Ball

The New Left in France: The Unified Socialist Party
Charles Hauss

The Tragedy of Chile
Robert J. Alexander

The Communist Parties of Western Europe: A Comparative Study
R. Neal Tannahill

Political philosophy as therapy————

MARCUSE RECONSIDERED

Gertrude A. Steuernagel

Contributions in Political Science, Number 11

GREENWOOD PRESS
WESTPORT, CONNECTICUT • LONDON, ENGLAND

JA
74
.5
.S78
Sp 2

Library of Congress Cataloging in Publication Data

Steuernagel, Gertrude A
   Political philosophy as therapy.

   (Contributions in political science ; no. 11
ISSN 0147-1066)
   Bibliography: p.
   Includes index.
   1. Political psychology. 2. Political science.
3. Marcuse, Herbert, 1898-   —Political science.
4. Jung, Carl Gustav, 1875-1961. I. Title.
JA74.5.S76   320'.01'9   78-73790
ISBN 0-313-20315-6

Library of Congress Catalog Card Number: 78-73790
ISBN: 0-313-20315-6
ISSN: 0147-1066

First published in 1979

Greenwood Press, Inc.
51 Riverside Avenue, Westport, Connecticut 06880

Printed in the United States of America

10 9 8 7 6 5 4 3 2 1

Copyright Acknowledgments

An earlier version of Chapter 4 appeared as "The Revitalization of Political Philosophy: Towards a Marcuse-Jung Synthesis," *Polity*, vol. 10, no. 3 (Spring 1978): 365-378. The chapter is used here with the permission of the editor.

For my father and in memory of my mother

Contents

Preface

The task of political philosophy is to articulate the political meaning of reality, to make intelligible the political significance of events, and to help us to understand the consequences of acting politically. There are many approaches to the study of political philosophy, and each approach emphasizes a particular aspect of the discipline. No single approach can claim exclusivity, but the combination of various approaches can expand our understanding of political reality.

This study will focus on a particular approach, what will be referred to as political philosophy as therapy. It is no more or no less valid than any of the more traditional approaches. Its strength is one of focus; political philosophy as therapy explores the relationship between self and the political dimension, between internal and external reality. Those who work in this mode use psychoanalytic concepts; they attempt to apply what we know about the unconscious to how we think about politics. Most of these have turned to Freud for their concepts and vocabulary; but a case will be made that it is Jung, the founder of analytical psychology, whose ideas are more compatible with the tasks of political philosophy. Herbert Marcuse, a contemporary political philosopher, has been chosen as the vehicle for the development of this approach.

Gertrude A. Steuernagel

POLITICAL PHILOSOPHY
AS THERAPY

Introduction

A metaphor or analogy must prove its worth; it is necessary to demonstrate that something can be learned by using it, something that cannot be gained by exclusive reliance upon exposition or description. The metaphor of political philosophy as therapy and the political philosopher as therapist is useful. More can be learned about the nature and functions of political philosophy and the role of the political philosopher by using this metaphor than by attempting to construct yet another description of the discipline and the role of those who practice it.

It is not a distortion of the discipline to conceive of political philosophy as therapy. The roots of the therapeutic function of political philosophy can be traced to what Pedro Lain Entralgo refers to as the "therapy of the word." Entralgo, in his brilliant work of the same name, traces the development of the therapy of the word in classical antiquity, following the early recognition of the therapeutic potential of the word from the Homeric epic through Socrates, the Sophists, Plato, Hippocrates, and Aristotle.

Entralgo dispels the notion that the ancient physicians had a purely natural conception of therapy. He notes their awareness of the connection of the body and the soul and their consequent recognition that physical health, in some instances, can be achieved through the use of words.

This connection between human disease and the power of the word was particularly evident in the Homeric epic. Entralgo discusses three ways in which the epic used verbal expression in the

therapeutic manner: as a charm, as a plea for health which had
the form of a prayer to the gods, and as a "persuasive and strength-
ening conversation with the patient."[1] The third use, in particular,
is significant for Entralgo's argument. He sees it as an example of
the epic's conscious awareness of the therapeutic capacity of human
speech. It represents, from his perspective, a movement away from
magical and prayer uses to an almost natural use of the word in a
therapeutic situation. In this case, the words are not directed to a
demon or god who may be causing the illness but, rather, to the
person who is directly experiencing the suffering. The focus is
shifted away from factors other than the word, the speaker, and
the hearer; there is no dependence on a transcendent source. As
Entralgo notes, this "cheering speech" is directed to the person as
an individual: "The therapist in this case speaks so that his words,
by acting upon the nature of the patient, may produce in it an
effect natural to them."[2]

According to Entralgo, the period following the time of the
Homeric epic until Plato was a time of change both culturally and
in respect to the use of the word as therapy. There was a change
from what Dodds called the shame culture to the guilt culture,
which was reflected in a change in the conception and treatment
of disease. Disease in this period, referred to as the Greek Middle
Ages, was seen as punishment for personal fault. The Greeks used
both empirical and magico-religious medicine, but their reliance
on the persuasive power of the word reflected the predominant
role of speech overall in the culture.[3]

The word was seen as superior to force. "Words, vigorous and
persuasive words; they are the key to interhuman relation and
success in the city."[4] Words "have the ability to achieve the cure
of human disease or at least to help in it."[5] If sickness is seen as a
violent disorder of the passions, then the word can cure and com-
fort.

The Sophists continued the development of the therapeutic
function of persuasion. Gorgias argued that the word "acts upon
the soul as medicaments upon the body."[6] The rhetor, according
to Entralgo, may have been a more able therapist than the physician, particularly when the symptoms involved grief and sorrow.
Specifically, verbal persuasion, acting according to the causes,
succeeds in eliminating pain from the mind: the thought and the

word of the curative rhetorician, his *logos*, set in order and rationalize the psychic and physical life of the sufferer.[7]

Entralgo goes on to argue that Plato himself was aware of the power of the word as charm. He believed that words could produce a condition of *sophrosyne*. Plato, according to Entralgo, was "the *inventor of a rigorously technical verbal psychotherapy*."[8] Entralgo argues:

> Gorgias and Antiphon are but prehistory beside Plato. Thanks to his vigorous and subtle rationalizing endeavor the old therapeutic epode, the magic charm or conjuration of ancient times, is resolved into three elements very different from one another. The magical, the rational, and the beseeching.[9]

The Hippocratic texts presented a deviation from the culture of words that had characterized the previous period. In the earlier times words as political as well as therapeutic instruments dominated the culture. In the time of the Hippocratic texts the therapeutic function of words was limited to winning the patient's confidence and maintaining his spirit.[10] The texts, according to Entralgo, are almost silent on the therapeutic function of the word; they rejected the charm in favor of physiological medicine and saw human beings solely in somatic terms. They advanced science; but, as Entralgo observes, this was not done without some sacrifice: "The incapacity of Western medicine for verbal psychotherapy until a few decades ago depended ultimately on that great achievement and that great limitation of Hippocratic medicine."[11]

Entralgo finds in Aristotle, however, a "speculative theory of verbal psychotherapy."[12] Aristotle, according to Entralgo, although he inherited and contradicted the use of the word as therapy, did understand the action of persuasion on the soul. Aristotle's death, for Entralgo, signified the end of the era of the therapy of the word in classical antiquity.

NOTES

1. Pedro Lain Entralgo, *The Therapy of the Word in Classical Antiquity*, trans. L.J. Rather and John M. Sharp (New Haven: Yale University Press, 1970), p. 23.

2. Ibid., p. 30.
3. Ibid., p. 67.
4. Ibid., p. 68.
5. Ibid., p. 69.
6. Ibid., p. 93.
7. Ibid., p. 104.
8. Ibid., p. 126.
9. Ibid.
10. Ibid., p. 163.
11. Ibid., p. 170.
12. Ibid., p. 174.

CHAPTER 1

Political Philosophy As Therapy

The metaphor of political philosophy as therapy can be developed by turning first to Sheldon Wolin's discussion of political philosophy and then to C.G. Jung's conception of therapy.

Wolin's discussion of political philosophy emphasizes the diagnostic and curative functions of the discipline. In the first chapter of *Politics and Vision*, Wolin argues that political philosophy is difficult to define because it is "not an essence with an eternal nature" but, rather, "a complex activity which is to be understood by analyzing the many ways that the acknowledged masters have practiced it."[1] Political philosophy, according to Wolin, is public; it is concerned with those things which concern all the members of a community, and those who engage in political philosophy are linked by their sharing in a continuity of considerations which define the subject itself.

Political philosophy, he contends, is both historical and transcendent; it is reflective of the perceptions of those who engage in it and something beyond their perceptions. It is something that emerges out of the times, but it can influence those times. "The boundaries of what is political have been shifting ones," he notes; but one must remember that "the field of politics is and has been, in a significant and radical sense, a created one."[2] Although Wolin contends that he does not mean to imply that "the political philosopher has been at liberty to call 'political' whatever he chose," he does argue that the designation of certain activities and arrangements as political, the characteristic way that we think about them, and the concepts we employ to communicate our observations and reactions—none of these are written into the nature of things but are the legacy accruing from the historical activity of political philosophers.[3]

The political philosopher is one who makes sense of political facts. It is the "concepts and categories," as Wolin calls them, of the political philosopher which "impart some order to what might otherwise appear to be a hopeless chaos of activities."[4] In addition, these concepts and categories "mediate between us and the political world we seek to render intelligible; they create an area of determinate awareness and thus help to separate the relevant phenomena from the irrelevant."[5]

Wolin's discussion of political philosophy and the task of the political philosopher reflect his conception of politics itself, which he sees as characterized by this same dynamic, changing nature, but which is limited by certain given boundaries. He notes that politics is the expression of society's need to readjust. The philosopher's concern for order reflects recognition of this attempt at order. "Politics," according to Wolin, "is both a source of conflict and a mode of activity that seeks to resolve our conflicts and promote readjustment."[6] The task of the political philosopher is to make known these conflicts through concepts and categories, to articulate and to offer possible cures for the disorders, and to guide with a vision of order. To perform this task, political philosophers use a particular vocabulary, a certain set of words. In addition, a key element of the "vision" of political philosophers is their use of imagination or fancy, something which helps them to "render political phenomena intellectually manageable," to present them in a "corrected fullness."[7] Imagination is critical to political philosophers since they, like all of us, are prevented from seeing a direct comprehensive picture: "The impossibility of direct observation compels the theorist to epitomize a society by abstracting certain phenomena and providing interconnections where none can be seen. Imagination is the theorist's means for understanding a world he can never 'know' in an intimate way."[8] Imagination, for Wolin, becomes the theorist's way of transcending history; and it is not, in his argument, something that detracts from the validity of the philosopher's enterprise. Wolin refused to concede that political philosophy is unscientific because its propositions, language, and reliance upon imagination lack empirical vigor or testability. His argument is that such a charge, even if valid in respect to most cases, is not a "conclusive objection"; that is, it is not something that calls into question the validity of the task itself. It is Wolin's contention that there are methods other than empirical tests for determining the meaningfulness of a statement. He contends that political theory belongs "to a different form of discourse" and turns to Carnap's conception of explication to develop his point: "Explication employs meanings that are less precise than those ideally suited for rigorous discussion, yet they are handy and, when redefined and rendered more precise, can perform extremely useful service in a theory."[9] For Wolin, political theory has many explicative concepts.

In summary, Wolin's political philosopher uses a specialized language to diagnose chaos and proposes, through his vision, recommendations that will bring order out of that chaos. Disease is seen as chaos, a lack of order, and health as order. His curative tools are his words, particularly those which help to suggest how the chaos came to be. He argues that political philosophers have been intent on "posting warnings" and that political philosophy "tries to state the necessary and sufficient conditions for attaining ends which, for one reason or another, are deemed good or desirable."[10]

JUNG AND PSYCHOTHERAPY

If one single theme emerges from Jung's writings it is his insistence on the need to consider all theories and therapeutic practices. Jung refutes those who claim any kind of exclusive status for their ideas and practices just as he refutes those therapists who speak from the seat of authority rather than as human beings. It is Jung's contention that the psyche itself is so diverse, so complex, that there must be many theories to deal with it.

The treatment must be individualized, that is, it must be shaped to fit the needs of the patient and his particular problems. To do

this, a therapist must remain free of prejudice and open and receptive to all forms of theories and practices. As Jung notes, "In dealing with psychological developments, the doctor should, as a
matter of principle, let nature rule and himself do his utmost to
avoid influencing the patient in the direction of his own philosophical, social, and political bent."[11] This becomes a problem for the
therapist when the patient is dealing with what Jung calls a "collective problem." In the course of this treatment, the patient may
engage in philosophical questions, questions that force the therapist
himself to engage in a discussion of the meaning of life and reevalu-
ate his own goals and ideals. Jung says that therapists should be,
are in fact, philosophers or philosophic doctors. It is his hope that
the therapist, who must be healthy, will remain open so that he
won't be tempted to impose his goals on the patient. The goals
that the patient finally settles on, he argues, must be those "that
best correspond to the patient's emotional state."[12]

This is not to say that Jung operates without any theoretical
preference. He does have a vision of health, and it is this vision
that guides him in his therapeutic practice. Individual health, or
individuation, is a process of complementing or compensating.
An unhealthy individual is one who is dominated by the unconscious or the conscious side of his personality, and it is Jung's task
to attempt a reintegration.

The dialectical nature of Jung's theories and practices is evident.
His goal is not a static state but a form of order that is based on
balance. Therapy is a process of continual readjustment to internal
and external needs. According to Jung, its "principal aim . . . is not
to transport the patient to an impossible state of happiness, but to
help him acquire steadfastness and philosophic patience in face of
suffering. Life demands for its completion and fulfillment a balance
between joy and sorrow."[13] The patient must adapt not only to
the demands of his own reality, his internal reality, but also to the
demands of the external world, for "Try as we may to concentrate
on the most personal problems, our therapy nevertheless stands or
falls with the question: What sort of world does our patient come
from and to what sort of world has he to adapt himself?"[14] Jung,
however, is aware of the individual's need to maintain himself as an
individual at the same time he makes the necessary adaptations.

The important thing, from Jung's perspective, is that the individual remain an individual, which signifies that the person retains a conscious free will and freedom of choice. Jung's own words convey his thoughts on this subject most graphically:

> If, then, man cannot exist without society, neither can he exist without oxygen, water, albumen, fat, and so forth. Like these, society is one of the necessary conditions of his existence. It would be ludicrous to maintain that man lives in order to breathe air. It is equally ludicrous to say that the individual exists for society. "Society" is nothing more than a term, a concept for the symbiosis of a group of human beings. A concept is not the carrier of life. The sole and natural carrier of life is the individual, and that is so throughout nature.[15]

So, although Jung does admit that the individual is a social being and that he must make all the adjustments that this demands, he sees the important unit as the individual, not the society or the state.[16] Jung's vision for man is a collective vision, because his conception of man is collective ("Individuation is an at-one-ment with oneself and at the same time with humanity, since oneself is a part of humanity"); but he is opposed to an "anonymous mass" and prefers a "conscious community" composed of individuals with "conscious freedom of choice and individual decision."[17]

CONCLUSIONS

The parallels between Wolin's conception of political philosophy and Jung's conception of therapy are obvious. Here the metaphor proves its worth, for it is possible to learn a great deal about political philosophy and its task from it.

Wolin and Jung both emphasize the fluid nature of their disciplines. Wolin's "complex activity" is equivalent to Jung's "dialectical conversation." Neither political philosophy nor therapy can be thought of as static, codified disciplines. Even Jung, the founder of the new science of analytical psychology, was quick to argue that he laid claim to no universal or exclusive validity for his ideas. Wolin seems to be saying much the same thing, and this becomes extremely critical for the task of political philosophy. To conceive

of political philosophy as therapy means to be alive to the complex
and often intricate demands of internal and external reality. It
means being willing to fit the type of political recommendations to
the reality we are confronted with rather than trying to impose a
series of principles on a community or group of individuals. Jung
argues that different theories of the psyche and different psycho-
therapeutic techniques are good for different people. He even goes
so far at times as to recommend a religious or even political solution
if he thinks it fits best.[18] The political philosopher as therapist must
heed Jung's warning and realize that the vision of health, although
it may contain certain absolutes, must be tailored to fit the community with which the philosopher is dealing. Wolin echoes this
warning when he argues that what characterizes political philosophy is not a continuity of solutions but a continuity of preoc-
cupations. Wolin has noted that each theorist has viewed political
reality from a different perspective or vision. The different perspectives of the theorists involve matters of selection and focus as
well as emphasis. One of the resulting problems has always been,
according to Wolin, the defining of what is political, the need to
include all that should be included and all that should be excluded.
This problem is also something that concerns Jung, particularly
when he tries to define what is psychological and what is philosophical and religious. Wolin, like Jung, agrees that the boundaries that decide what is political and not political have been
shifting ones. The philosopher as well as the therapist often, in
effect, creates what is political and what is psychological by using
concepts and categories to designate certain phenomena.

Jung traces the long process of psychotherapy's development out
of the medical faculties (here his analysis closely parallels that
of Entralgo). In many ways, psychic phenomena became psychic
phenomena because the therapist was able to make them such by
attaching a label to them. Wolin continually makes the point that
much of what is political is what is created. This contention has
important implications for our ways of thinking about politics.
Political space is created space. It involves both the transcendent
and the historical, the universal and the particular.

Wolin notes that the concept of political space illustrates "the
metaphysical categories resident in political theory" and includes

"the crucial question of the arrangements for settling the problems arising out of the fact that a large number of human beings, possessing a common cultural identity, occupies the same determinate area."[19]

The political philosopher as therapist is confronted with another type of political space, the collective unconscious and the collective consciousness of a society and the individuals who compose it. Just as "political space becomes a problem when human energies cannot be controlled by existing arrangements," so do the collective unconscious and collective conscious become a problem when the individual or the society is unable to cope with disturbances in them. [20] Here, too, the intermingling of the personal and political becomes a key element. Psychological problems can be political problems, and political problems can be psychological.

It is possible to learn something about the role of the political philosopher as therapist by reading Jung. The political philosopher, like the therapist, has a healing function. Both are concerned, ultimately, with a form of order or balance. As Wolin has noted, "No political theorist has ever advocated a disordered society, and no political theorist has ever proposed permanent revolution as a way of life."[21]

What is order or balance for Jung, and what is the role of the therapist in achieving it? Health, for Jung, is "individuation," a condition in which there is a balance between the unconscious and conscious aspects of the individual's personality. Wolin has noted that "most of the great statements of political philosophy have been put forward in times of crisis."[22] The therapist, too, is spurred to action when confronted with a crisis in the patient's life. The crises are similar; they are generally crises of adaptation, a failure of society to readjust to changing economic conditions, for example, and a failure of consciousness to adjust to changes in the unconscious or the external reality. When Wolin talks about crisis, he refers to the time when "political phenomena are less effectively integrated by institutional forms."[23] Likewise, when consciousness is unable to deal with reality, new forms or new ways of dealing with it can come (prompted by the therapist) from the unconscious.

But here Jung's warnings become even more critical. In discussing the problems of the patient, he notes that adequate attention must be paid to the individual as well as the social dimensions of existence. This point was made very clearly in the earlier discussion of Jung. The therapist must guard against universal solutions to particular problems. So must the political philosopher. Wolin is aware that the problems of the political philosopher are often shaped by the times themselves; but he also recognizes that there are certain universals which concern the political philosopher. The philosopher, like the therapist, can be guided by the universals but must be careful not to eliminate the particular or the individual. Likewise, concern for the historical must not override the transcendent.

This is not to say that the lesson the political philosopher should take from Jung is to ignore the social or the collective elements in our nature. What Wolin calls the "communal nature" of political knowledge has an important parallel in Jung's theories and practices. One of Jung's major tenets is that the patient must be made aware that his suffering is not unique, that his isolation or sense of it is unwarranted, and that he shares a common bond with others. The individual's problems are shown to be a part of something that everyone shares, and he is encouraged to explore the collective nature of his psyche. The neurotic can be cured by recognizing the collective. Jung argues that there are two groups of psychoneuroses: "the one comprising collective people with underdeveloped individuality, the other individualists with atrophied collective adaptation."[24] The dialectic procedure is all-important because of the presence of collectivity and individuality.

What about the political philosopher as therapist? Jung is most informative in those respects. The therapist for Jung is human. This point is simple, but it is often overlooked in schools of thought which caution that the analyst should not express emotion or feeling to the patient but, rather, should speak with the voice of authority. The analyst, for Jung, uses certain concepts and categories to overcome the isolation of the individual and to offer an alternative vision. The therapist does not remain separate from the patient; he expands the patient's understanding of his psyche through interpretation and the addition of other materials, but he does not speak from an infallible seat of authority. The therapist does have a vision of health, but it is not drawn out of thin air. It is a combination of the individual's life and the therapist's knowledge of the workings of the psyche. It is the able therapist who is capable of turning to his own knowledge and ideas to understand the reality of the patient. Jung spurns the notion that the therapist must spend an endless amount of time with the patient and that the patient must depend totally upon the therapist's knowledge. Jung thinks that one or two hours a week are sufficient for the therapeutic encounter. What he attempts to do is give the patient enough knowledge to work on his own between visits. He does not, for instance, think that transference is a necessary part of the treatment.

Finally, imagination plays a role in the work of the therapist and the political philosopher. Even though their concepts and language might lack empirical vigor, they are not invalid.

SUMMARY

Political philosophy, for Wolin, was a "complex activity" rather than an enterprise with some kind of eternal essence. This appraisal is characteristic of Jung's view of psychotherapy. He argues continually that psychotherapy is helpful only if it is conceived of as a dialectic, as a conversation between the therapist and the patient. The Jungian therapist, like Wolin's political philosopher, is concerned with a communal subject. One of the major tenets of Jung's thought is the need to overcome the isolation of the individual, to demonstrate that what he might conceive of as an individual and particular experience is actually communal and universal. A key to Jungian therapy is making the individual recognize the collective nature of his problems, defining them as something common to each of us because they involve psychic processes that we all share. A corollary is Jung's belief that the therapist will fail if he attempts to impose a series of tenets on the patient's individual case. Jungian therapy, in this sense, like Wolin's political philosophy, involves elements of the historical and the transcendent; and it is the skillful therapist who can adapt the transcendent elements of the therapy to the patient's reality. What the therapist does, equivalent to the political philosopher, is to use concepts and categories that make the psychological reality meaningful for the patient. The therapist is not giving answers; he too is suggesting an alternative vision, a way to interpret complex phenomena. The therapist deals with the political space of the unconscious, adjusting the continual demands of the psyche, seeking a readjustment between the conscious and unconscious dimensions of existence. The therapist will not always use concepts and categories which will withstand empirical tests, his key concepts such as archetypes are excluded almost by definition, but he does try to use language that will explicate the phenomena.

EXAMPLES

Thomas Spragens, Jr., and James M. Glass, both heavily influenced by Sheldon Wolin, are most direct in their understanding of the therapeutic function of political philosophy.

Spragens writes explicitly of the therapeutic function of political philosophy. He does not claim exclusivity for his work but sees his task as contributing to "the understanding and appreciation of political theory."[25] He focuses on Plato, Hobbes, and Rousseau, whose works, he contends, "attempt to provide a profound and relatively comprehensive vision of political life"; and he strives to unfold the elements of their visions.[26] A political theorist, from his perspective, writes not only to satisfy himself but also in the hope that his message will be heeded. A political theory, then, becomes an attempt to reorient the members of society, for "The task, the hope, the promise of political theory is to deliver us from this failure of vision and therefore from the 'repressiveness' of our social arrangements."[27] "In many respects, in fact," he continues,

political theory can be characterized as a kind of psychotherapy of the body politic. The analogy is a good one in respect to both the structure and the purpose of the inquiry. Like psychotherapy, political theory necessitates a deep exploration of the roots of human behavior—areas which have for so long been tacit and taken for granted that they lie beneath the usual range of consciousness. And, like psychotherapy, the ultimate goal of political theory is the restoration of health through confrontation with and triumph over the sources of distress.[28]

Glass's work gives witness to what Frank calls an attempt to "heal through persuasion."[29] Frank notes that there is always a "personal relationship between healer and sufferer" and that "certain types of therapy rely primarily on the healer's ability to mobilize healing forces in the sufferer by psychological means."[30] Frank contends that psychotherapy has the following elements, and it is these factors that Glass identifies in his reexamination of the classics:

1. A trained, socially sanctioned healer, whose healing powers are accepted by the sufferer and by his social group or an important segment of it.
2. A sufferer who seeks relief from the healer.
3. A circumscribed, more or less structured series of contacts between the healer and the sufferer, through which the healer, often with the aid of a group, tries to produce certain changes in the sufferer's emotional state, attitudes, and behavior.[31]

One theme that permeates much of Glass's work is the therapeutic role of the political philosopher. In one of his essays, Glass likens the political philosopher to the shaman. He argues that such philosophers as Rousseau, Marx, and Plato have used their philosophical visions much as the shaman uses his incantations, to attempt a cure that will overcome the suffering of the patient. According to Glass's analogy, the philosopher's concepts are the functional equivalent of the shaman's images. Extending the comparison, Glass contends that both the philosopher and the shaman make their curative statements for public purposes. Each offers a regenerative vision with the intent of offering a cure for the suffering of alienated existence; and both attempt to remedy an atrophied reality by appealing to another, unconscious level of existence which will "heal" the destructiveness of history. Both the shaman and the philosopher, according to Glass, attempt to transform consciousness; and both attempt to have their alternative vision internalized in the hope that this vision will replace, and thereby heal, the destructiveness of the non-vital image held in its place. History, or the present reality, is, in Glass's view, the villain for both the philosopher and the shaman. The philosopher attempts to tap an ahistorical, unconscious dimension that will

bring unity where heretofore there has been only chaos. The unconscious, as Glass argues, is important for both the philosopher
and the shaman; it represents something outside of historical consciousness. Glass, unlike some others in this mode, finds Jung's
concept of the unconscious particularly helpful in establishing a
realm independent of consciousness.

The task of the philosopher is a communal one; he works
through the individual to cure the community, for "To free his
body and consciousness of sickness means to redeem the entire
physical and perceptual orientation of the community."[32] The
philosopher must demystify the power of the disease-causing
structures; he must argue that their existence is not preordained
or natural. What is natural for Glass is what is personal and individual; it is political reality or, rather, a particular form of political reality which he sees as destructive. Thus the existence of
another dimension is critical to his argument; the vision of regeneration cannot come from that same dimension which is so
destructive to the self. Glass, although he does not cite Entralgo,
speaks in terms that echo the latter's description of the therapy of
the word:

> The philosophical incantation, as a psychological cure, possesses a
> meaning which transcends formal classifications, whether "descriptive"
> or normative; it enters into consciousness, ideally as a transformer of
> meaning, as a perceptual magic that banishes the historical causes of
> suffering and founds an entirely novel gestalt.[33]

The philosopher, Glass's "external agent," introduces the vision
to the consciousness of the listener as an "alternative scheme for
arranging psychic and physical facts."[34] Like the shaman, the
philosopher hopes that conceptual psychotherapy will be understood and accepted by the audience, the community.

Glass turns to Rousseau to confirm the existence of a therapeutic
dimension in the work of that philosopher. He argues that the
therapeutic function of Rousseau's work acknowledges that "no
change made sense unless it was accompanied by a radical altera-
tion in the nature of feeling, response, and most particularly
the use and purposes of the instruments of social exchange."[35] It
is Rousseau who, according to Glass, mediates between knowl-

edge and self. It is Glass's argument that now that we have the tools to better understand the self and its relationship to political reality, we can apply these concepts to some of the pre-psychological thinkers. Again he notes that the philosopher has to speak to the unconscious as well as the conscious in an attempt to cure. To do therapy means to be able to reach this unconscious dimension, and he sees in Rousseau the recognition of a need for a dimension apart from the historical one which is responsible for the individual's suffering. Rousseau's vision, according to Glass, is one which "reaches into the self; it penetrates the 'being' of the person and ultimately transforms all existing *gestalt*."[36]

The task of the philosopher is to induce a vision, a form of incantation, which will counteract the reality which is destroying what is natural. Philosophy, according to Glass, possesses a power to intervene, to inject itself into that alienated existence, and to infuse an atrophied reality with new energy.

Again it is the natural for Glass which is good and the social, or a particular form of socially acquired possessiveness, which is bad. The philosopher has to attempt to tap what is within the individual in order to cure him. As Glass notes:

Before natural man finds himself corrupted by social possessiveness (the encircling of self in property), he contains within his being the potentiality to experience a feeling unrelated to anything social. It is this quality which for the philosopher-therapist stands at the heart of reconstructing the consciousness or ego of the natural man.[37]

Glass once more turns to his metaphor of the philosopher as shaman and notes the similarity between the task of the philosopher-therapist and that of the shaman:

For the philosopher-therapist, the critical task of theory lies in devising a set of prescriptions of concepts that while appealing to consciousness also possess the almost shamanic power of reaching into the unconscious and fundamentally changing the affect structures with the self.[38]

According to Glass, the "legislator" becomes Rousseau's surrogate transformer; and "The making of the *Contract* acts as the critical bridge leading the natural self to a developed and fulfilling con-

sciousness dependent on a community whose origin bears no relationship to the division of labor or the historical process."[39]

The metaphor of political philosophy as therapy dominates
Glass's work. His conception of the political philosopher as shaman, a theme that recurs throughout his essays, allows him to
focus in on what he believes to be the central task of political
philosophy: the suggestion and implementation of vision (through
the action on consciousness and the unconscious) which will cure
the disease of atrophied historical consciousness. He not only
claims that this is the primary task of the political philosopher
but argues that the evidence for such a conception can be found
in the work of many of the masters. His interpretation of Rousseau,
in particular, is used to support his theory; and it is easy to see
that Glass not only advances his own theory by the use of this
example but contributes a new, striking interpretation of Rousseau.
Glass continually emphasizes what he refers to as "the capacity of
philosophic knowing to transcend the corrosive effects of historical
process."[40]

Glass's article on Machiavelli and alchemical transformation
brings further support to his argument. He contends that alchemical theory, when examined from a Jungian perspective, can give
new insight into the meaning of the *Prince*. In this essay, Glass
likens the alchemist to a therapist and the political philosopher
to an alchemist, united around an attempt "to redeem an almost
hopelessly depraved human situation."[41] Here again, consistent
with the other essays, Glass argues that the transformation must
occur through an agency independent of the dominant reality,
a recognition which he finds in Machiavelli's work: "Further, like
the alchemical *opus*, Machiavelli's conception of a redeemed
political environment relies heavily on the singular and total power
of a transforming agency which seems to be independent of con-
straints conditioning normal or conventional exchange and
value."[42] Both the alchemist and the political philosopher, according to Glass, tap Jungian archetypes. Again his theme of history
as villain comes to the fore as he notes that the energy coming from
this ahistorical dimension has the power to cure the destructiveness
of historical reality. Machiavelli, he notes, like the alchemist,
"attacks convention and perverse historical forms."[43] Machiavelli
seeks to rediscover "political vitality, those first or primary prin-

ciples that made political life more than a self-interested lusting after power" and attempts to effect "a kind of collective experience moving a political community closer to its roots in a common past."[44] The Prince becomes the symbol of the curing agency; and his action "symbolizes the archetype of rebirth."[45]

SUMMARY

What is common to Glass and Spragens is the application of psychoanalytic concepts to the study of the classics, but their work does not stop there. Not only do they attempt to understand political reality in psychoanalytic terms and apply psychoanalytic categories to the theories they survey, but they argue that certain philosophers have this notion of the therapeutic function of political philosophy and that it is fruitful to look at these theories from the vantage point of our more developed psychoanalytic theories so as to better understand exactly what it was they were trying to do.

Marcuse becomes an excellent vehicle for the further development of this approach. Not only does he attempt to bring a healthy order out of chaos through the use of his vision, a function of the political philosopher as therapist, but he self-consciously turns to psychoanalytic concepts and language to assist him.

NOTES

1. Sheldon S. Wolin, *Politics and Vision* (Boston: Little, Brown and Company, 1960), pp. 1-2.

2. Ibid., p. 4-5.

3. Ibid., p. 5.

4. Ibid., p. 6.

5. Ibid.

6. Ibid., p. 11.

7. Ibid., p. 19.

8. Ibid.

9. Ibid.

10. Ibid., p. 13.

11. C.G. Jung, *The Practice of Psychotherapy*, trans. R.F.C. Hull, Bollingen Series 20 (New York: Pantheon Books, 1954), p. 26.

12. Ibid., p. 80.

13. Ibid., p. 81.

14. Ibid., p. 95.

15. Ibid., p. 106.

16. Ibid., pp. 104-105; for Jung's attacks on society and the State, see in particular ibid., pp. 106-107, and the *Undiscovered Self.*

17. *Practice of Psychotherapy*, p. 108.

18. Ibid., pp. 16-17.

19. Wolin, *Politics and Vision*, p. 16.

20. Ibid., p. 17.

21. Ibid., p. 8.

22. Ibid.

23. Ibid.

24. Jung, *Practice of Psychotherapy*, p. 7.

25. Thomas A. Spragens, Jr., *Understanding Political Theory* (New York: St. Martin's Press, 1976), p. *v.*

26. Ibid., p. 1.

27. Ibid., p. 8.

28. Ibid., p. 29.

29. Jerome D. Frank, *Persuasion and Healing* (Baltimore: The Johns Hopkins Press, 1961), p. *x.*

30. Ibid., p. 1.

31. Ibid., pp. 2-3.

32. James M. Glass, "The Philosopher and the Shaman: The Political Vision as Incantation," *Political Theory* 2 (May 1974), p. 190.

33. Ibid., p. 193.

34. Ibid.

35. James M. Glass, "Political Philosophy as Therapy: Rousseau and the Pre-Social Origins of Consciousness," *Political Theory* 4 (May 1976), p. 164.

36. Ibid., pp. 165-66.

37. Ibid., p. 174.

38. Ibid., p. 177.

39. Ibid., pp. 178-79.

40. Ibid., p. 181.

41. James M. Glass, "Machiavelli's Prince and Alchemical Transformation: Action and the Archetype of Regeneration," *Polity* 8 (Summer 1976), p. 504.

42. Ibid., pp. 504-505.

43. Ibid., p. 510.

44. Ibid., p. 515-16.

45. Ibid., p. 523.

CHAPTER 2

Marcuse Reconsidered

Marcuse was born in Berlin, Germany, in 1898. He left Germany in 1933; and in 1934, after a year in Geneva, he emigrated to the United States and began work at the Institute of Social Research at Columbia University. Marcuse, along with Max Horkheimer and T. W. Adorno, was a founder of the Frankfurt school of Marxist sociology. Martin Jay's *Dialectical Imagination* traces the development of the Frankfurt school and situates Marcuse's thought in relation to that of his contemporaries.[1]

Marcuse is the author of many books and articles. Two of the more complete bibliographies of his major and minor works can be had in *The Critical Spirit*, edited by Kurt H. Wolff and Barrington Moore, Jr., and *Herbert Marcuse: From Marx to Freud and Beyond*, by Sidney Lipshires.[2] In addition, Marcuse has been the subject of many interpretative articles, reviews, interviews, and dissertations.[3]

A brief review of some of the more recent interpretations of Marcuse's work should help the uninitiated reader to understand his thought and should aid the more advanced student in discovering possible topics for future research. Although the works selected for inclusion in this section are not necessarily the major interpretations of Marcuse, they do represent a cross section of the Marcusean literature.

Marcuse's critics are many. His attempt to synthesize Freud and Marx has placed him in the unenviable position of being attacked by Marxists for being too Freudian and by Freudians for being too Marxist. Several other critics conclude that he is simply muddle-headed, confused, or, at best, ambiguous. He has been attacked for misleading an entire generation, for causing the downfall of the morality of the youth of the world, and for being personally responsible for the failure of the revolution of the working class.

This latter accusation is perhaps most directly formulated and developed in Jack Woddis's *New Theories of Revolution*. Woddis decries any attempt to label Marcuse a Marxist. He feels that Marcuse's rejection of the working class, or what he reads as Marcuse's rejection of the working class, provides sufficient grounds to banish him from the ranks of "correct thinkers." Marcuse, as Woddis would have it, should declare himself to be what he really is behind his Marxist cloak—an elitist, albeit deluded, thinker. Marcuse mistakenly contends, according to Woddis, that it is the "outsiders" who are the carriers of revolutionary humanism and that it is now time to turn to the intellectuals and the students since the working class has betrayed its revolutionary roots. Woddis is clearly angry with Marcuse. He not only feels that Marcuse has failed to deal with the most important questions of advanced industrial society, but he believes that the way in which Marcuse has done so and the questions he does consider have made him a dangerous traitor. It is Marcuse and his way of thinking, according to Woddis, that lead others away from genuine revolutionary concerns and away from the working class.

What Woddis fails to understand, however, is this: Marcuse is not cheering (nor has he ever cheered) the demise of the working class as a revolutionary force. He argues, instead, that the evidence seems to indicate that the traditional working class is no longer the "subjective" agent of revolution and that it is more fruitful to identify the new agents of revolution in contemporary society rather than to bemoan the loss of the old. Marcuse's consideration of the Third World movements, students, and intellectuals is not a personal preference; it is, rather, from his perspective, a discovery of dialectical trends in contemporary society.

An interesting contrast to Woddis's interpretation can be found in Roszak's *Making of a Counter Culture*.[4] Roszak places Marcuse among the ranks of those who argue for the necessity of a therapeutic revolution. Alienation for Marcuse, as Roszak reads him, is primarily an oppression of consciousness, and so revolution must be conceived of as a liberation of consciousness. Instead of condemning Marcuse for straying from Marx, as Woddis does, Roszak lauds his bold explorations into this crucial area. In many ways, Roszak finds Marcuse a more progressive thinker than Marx, a thinker who is not afraid to deal with elements of existence that Marx dismissed. Thus "we find in Marcuse and Brown a supreme evaluation placed on exactly those cultural elements which Marx, with his compulsive hard-headedness, banished to the status of 'shadowy forms in the brain of men.' "[5] According to Roszak, Marcuse was able to go beyond class conflict to an analysis of the human body "seen as that perennial battlefield where the war of the instincts is waged."[6]

Roszak supports Marcuse's efforts because he, unlike Woddis, shares Marcuse's ideas on alienation. Alienation, for Roszak, is primarily psychic rather than sociological; "It is not a proprietary distinction that exists *between* men of different classes, but rather a disease that is rooted *inside* all men."[7] If anything, it is Brown who, Roszak feels, grasps more completely the concept of the nature of alienation. Marcuse, he feels, is still too dominated by external reality.

Marcuse may well have missed his real calling; he could have served as a symbol reuniting the radical left and liberals. Woddis attacked Marcuse for abandoning Marx, but Marcuse clearly violates Maurice Cranston's liberal sensibilities.

Cranston calls Marcuse's particular brand of thought "Anarcho-Marxism" and expresses his disdain for it by arguing that it contains the worst elements of anarchism and Marxism. Marcuse, according to Cranston, rates poorly as a technical philosopher and as a social observer. He contends that Marcuse's Marxism is not the Marxism of the Soviet Union but that his particular conception of Marxism is based on his "belief that Marxism has taken over from liberalism the principle that liberalism has forsaken, notably freedom and individualism."[8] Cranston contends that it is Marcuse who poses a threat to these values, not liberals. Marcuse has concluded that at certain historical times under certain circumstances we must exercise intolerance toward certain ideas. Cranston finds this view particularly distasteful and dangerous. He cannot accept the idea that undemocratic methods can result in the type of society he knows he wants and he thinks Marcuse at least claims to want. In this context, Marcuse's comments on violence are particularly upsetting to Cranston, who argues that a total rejection of violence is the only defensible position. Cranston levels bitter charges against Marcuse:

> For all his attacks on Stalinism, Marcuse himself is advocating the very things that make Stalinism odious. And let us not be led astray by Marcuse's constant avowal of his attachment to the idea of freedom; as Milton and Locke remarked in the seventeenth century, the people who talk most about liberty are frequently its greatest enemies.[9]

Some of the best interpretations of Marcuse have been done by those who focus on the influences of Marx and Freud on his work. Paul Robinson, for example, understands Marcuse in terms of what he refers to as the "Freudian Left," a radical movement within psychoanalysis. Marcuse, according to Robinson, shares with Trilling and Norman O. Brown the recognition that a critical element has always existed in Freud's work itself and, like the other two, sets as his task the exposition of this element through a focus on Freud's later, more speculative work.

Robinson divides Marcuse's work into pre- and post-Freudian periods. He notes that Marcuse "came" to Freud after 1955 and that this signaled a significant break with his earlier focus on Hegel and Marx, although he does admit that there is a continuity to much of Marcuse's thought. Robinson traces Marcuse's concern for the central role of consciousness to his insistence on its centrality in Marx. Marcuse, according to Robinson, refused to accept determinism or sociological reductionism as representative of Marx's beliefs on the role of consciousness in the historical process. Marcuse, according to Robinson, persisted in taking Marx beyond economic concerns and demonstrated that Marx's position was actually a concern for the overall human condition.

Robinson does not see *Eros and Civilization* as a repudiation of Marcuse's Marxism. Rather, he interprets it as an attempt to synthesize Freud and Marx, as a translation of "the unhistorical, psychological categories of Freud's thought into the eminently historical and political categories of Marxism."[10] Marcuse, Robinson contends, reinterprets Freud primarily through the introduction of the concepts of surplus repression and the performance principle.[11] However, when Robinson considers Marcuse's post-*Eros and Civilization* remarks on Freud, he concludes that Marcuse has returned to Marx, his first love. Robinson speculates that this change could be explained at least in part by the circumstances of the times. Marcuse returned to more directly political questions in a more directly political time. Robinson, unfortunately, sees some of Marcuse's thoughts in *One-Dimensional Man* as a reversal rather than a development of the ideas in *Eros and Civilization*.

The failure to grasp the dialectical nature of Marcuse's work has led others to error. Instead of seeing the development of his ideas, these critics see only ambiguity, confusion, and contradiction.

The work of Bhiku Parekh is an obvious example of the consequences of such an error. Parekh indicts Marcuse for what he considers to be the latter's "manicheism." Marcuse, contends Parekh, conceives of the ideal society as all good and the existing society as all evil. Parekh, in contrast, argues that no society can be either perfect or absolutely evil.[12] Marcuse's conception of reality is never Manichaean, and his vision of liberation can be achieved only through a dialectical process. Marcuse summarizes his position in an article in the *Partisan Review*:

> Capitalism constantly creates needs (must create needs) which it cannot satisfy within its own framework—*transcending needs*. It is only at the most advanced stages of capitalism, and on the ground of the *satisfaction* of basic needs, that transcending needs drive beyond the capitalist mode of production: reduction and eventual elimination of alienated labor; self-determination as the new way of life; new relationships between men and women, between the generations, between man and nature. In short: socialism as a *qualitatively* different society.[13]

It is the technological advances of modern industrial society which Marcuse cites as a necessary prerequisite for a non-repressive society. An elimination of scarcity as a prime definer of the human condition comes only with these technological advances. Marcuse states this position quite directly:

Their dialectical historical character demands the development of their content in accord with, and in contradiction to, the actual development of society. Such a theoretical development must, in order to be dialectical, derive the new stage from the preceding one, thus retaining the intent and impetus of the original concept.[14]

Marcuse, with his redefinition of the concept of utopia, is attempting to elaborate what he considers to be potentialities that have become realized in the concrete historical process.

Parekh also argues that Marcuse's epistemology is naive. Marcuse, according to Parekh, believes that it is possible to develop the idea of a new society free from any connections with the old society. Parekh counters that reason is socially and culturally acquired and is shaped and conditioned by the established reality. Again, this is a gross misunderstanding of Marcuse and the dialectic. Marcuse's critical theory of society attempts to develop ideas based on objective alternatives in man's potential. His idea of a new society is not totally free from connections with the old society; and his conception of reason is not sterile, as Parekh contends. Rather, it is transcendent and ordering. Parekh appears to view reason as a reflection of an institutional arrangement, something socially and culturally acquired without any element of transcendence or autonomy attached to the individual ego. Reason, as seen by Parekh, is synonymous with the prevailing consciousness of a society: an individual, then, could reflect but not order reality.

Marcuse, contends Parekh, has conceptions which "cannot provide a satisfactory theory of political action."[15] He concludes that Marcuse must abandon the use of any of the resources of the old society in the creation of a new society. Again, this criticism reflects a lack of comprehension of the nature and function of the dialectical method. The accusation that Marcuse fails to provide a theory of political action demonstrates, on Parekh's part, a failure to understand the Marxist conception of praxis. Marcuse does not suffer this same fault. As he notes:

The new sensibility has become, by this very token, *praxis*: it emerges in the struggle against violence and exploitation where this struggle is waged for essentially new ways and forms of life: negation of the entire *Establishment*, its morality, culture; affirmation of the right to build a society in which the abolition of poverty and toil terminates in a universe where the sensuous, the playful, the calm, and the beautiful become forms of existence and thereby the *Form* of the society itself.[16]

The interpretation which follows is important as a prelude to the remainder of this work. Since Marcuse will be the vehicle for the development of an approach, this interpretation presents the reader with an overview of his major ideas.

Any reader familiar with Marcuse's work may be prone to argue that there is a distinction between an "early" and a "late" Marcuse. Since to understand Marcuse is to understand his use of the dialectic, it is more fruitful to set aside this distinction and to approach his work itself dialectically, that is, to argue that a basic understanding of Marcuse's thought can be gained by regarding *Eros and Civilization* as a thesis, *One-Dimensional Man* as its antithesis, and *An Essay on Liberation* as the synthesis.

The major theme of *Eros and Civilization* is that a non-repressive civilization is possible. This thesis is a reformulation of Freud's major contention in *Civilization and Its Discontents*. For Freud, however, Eros and Thanatos are in irreconcilable conflict; and civilization, although repressive, is necessary for survival. Psychical development, both ontogenetically and phylogenetically, is the history of the repression and sublimation of primary instinctual energy. It is here, at the root of Freud's theory, that Marcuse becomes radical. For Marcuse, civilization without repression is possible because of the historical nature of human beings; the nature of man is historically acquired, not biologically determined.

In *Eros and Civilization*, Marcuse attempts to break the historical link between happiness as renunciation and freedom as domination. He reopens the discussion of civilization and repression on the basis of Freud's theory itself. The chapters in *Eros and Civilization* concerned with Orpheus and Narcissus and the aesthetic dimension are critical to an understanding of Marcuse's alternative to a repressive reality. In effect, these symbols of a non-repressive reality are Marcuse's attempt to place such an idea in the tradition of critical theory. Marcuse is arguing that such utopian speculation is actually an elucidation of historical potentialities derived from that which remains untouched by the dominant reality, that is, the power of fantasy.

Marcuse introduces the concepts of surplus repression and the performance principle as means of distinguishing between biological and sociohistorical realities. He defines surplus repression as that repression which is necessitated by the specific historical form of domination. This repression, above and beyond what Freud considered necessary for civilization, is a characteristic of modern industrial society. Marcuse contends that there is an "inner unreconciled tension in Freud's theory" that provides the basis for a theory of a free Eros which does not "preclude lasting civilized societal relationship" and that there is a possibility of a free Eros which is not irrevocably fused with the aggressive instinct.[17]

The performance principle is defined as the specific form of the reality principle in this society. Marcuse argues that the performance principle is linked to the stratification of society "according to the competitive economic performances of its members."[18] Not only does Marcuse argue that a free Eros is possible; he contends that, even in its undifferentiated form in this society, Eros does not have to be as strongly controlled as it is under the performance principle. It is now possible, he argues, to reduce the amount of instinctual energy spent in alienated labor. Freud's dialectic of civilization would end if the performance principle was recognized as a specific historical mode of the reality principle.

On another level, Marcuse argues that the classical conception of the development of the psyche as formulated by Freud is itself becoming outdated. Freud's conception of psychical development was premised on the notion of private space, or room for the individual to experience the differentiation of the ego from the id and the superego from the ego. According to Marcuse, this mental space is declining as the scope of society increases; and the superego is extending its control over consciousness as well as instincts. It is here, however, that Marcuse reaffirms his commitment to the dialectic: these changes in psychic structure point to a dialectic of civilization, and "The living links between the individual and his culture are loosened."[19] These are the "positive aspects of progressive alienation."[20]

Marcuse argues that the union of the phylogenetic-biological and the sociological factors in man's instinctual structure is now "unnatural." However, technological progress itself cannot eliminate alienated labor. Progressive alienation does increase the potential for freedom as the individual becomes removed from the realm of necessity. Reason becomes sensuous; the roots of the aesthetic experience reemerge, and repressive reason gives way to a rationality of gratification—the convergence of reason and happiness. This is the optimistic prediction which concludes *Eros and Civilization*.

SUMMARY

The aesthetic dimension can provide a material model for the possibility of a non-repressive civilization. The model is material since the basis for it is found in man himself, in his unconscious and his power of fantasy. Symbols can provide evidence of this non-repressive reality. Eros need not be subject to the repression Freud thought necessary. Marcuse attempts to demonstrate that Eros and Thanatos are historical modifications of the instincts. That which we call Thanatos, he argues, is a specific manifestation of a desire to relieve tension under the performance principle. The superego and the ego are becoming socialized not by the family but by the society. It is these very changes in the psychic structure themselves which hold out the possibility of breaking this history of domination.

The critical conclusion of *Eros and Civilization* is the optimistic belief in progressive alienation. The individual's links to his culture are loosened because the energy that would be invested in the development of an autonomous psyche is freed, and the individual no longer has to invest energy in cathecting. Rather, he introjects society. In *One-Dimensional Man*, this lack of private space becomes a negative rather than a positive force. The necessities for maintaining society become individual needs, and the whole is contained within and appears to be the very embodiment of Reason. For Marcuse, it is the embodiment of irrationality. The sensuous reason of *Eros and Civilization* gives way to a universal Reason; the link between reason and happiness is shattered by a Reason which "delivers the goods." A perverted Sartrian "project" can epitomize a particular historical mode of domination rather than a potential for freedom. Once the project has become exclusive, it becomes dominant, as appears to have happened with the project that is advanced industrial society.

In *One-Dimensional Man*, Marcuse argues that there are no longer "individuals" in the Freudian sense because Freud's developmental process presupposes a private space. For Freud, "introjection" designates the process by which an individual adopts external controls. Marcuse argues that the term *introjection* may be obsolete because this concept implies a "Self (Ego) [which] transposes the 'outer' into the 'inner.'"[21] Marcuse would substitute the word *mimesis* for *introjection*. He characterizes this as a process in which "The result is not adjustment but *mimesis:* an immediate identification of the individual with *his* society, and, through it, with the society as a whole."[22] The individual develops needs which have a societal content and function; that is, these needs can never be the individual's own but are the needs of a repressive reality. Repressive desublimation aids in the attainment of a condition Marcuse labels "The Happy Consciousness—the belief that the real is rational and that the system delivers the goods."[23] This condition is characterized by one-dimensionality in thought and behavior. The individual, because his rationality is not his own and the forces of domination have reached into his instinctual structure itself, has lost the critical spirit of the dialectic and can no longer conceive of or demand an alternative to his given sociohistorical reality.

In *Eros and Civilization*, technology, through the elimination of scarcity, appeared as a potential for liberation. In *One-Dimensional Man*, it becomes irrational to criticize technology—that from which all that is good and pleasurable flows. Marcuse links the concept of totalitarian with the idea of domination, with the definition of the particular by the universal. For this society, irrationality is rational because it delivers the goods; therefore, opposition seems to be irrational.

Marcuse argues that two-dimensional culture is being "liquidated." Those elements which stood in opposition to the established reality, including the cultural elements, are being absorbed by the one-dimensional society. These cultural values, now produced on a mass scale, serve as instruments of social cohesion. Sexuality becomes liberalized in socially constructive forms. Repressive desublimation (mentioned in the preface added in 1961 to

Eros and Civilization and elaborated upon in *One-Dimensional Man)* appears as the converse of non-repressive sublimation. The latter process involves a revitalized Eros: "The sexual impulses, without losing their erotic energy, transcend their immediate object and eroticize normally non- and anti-erotic relationships between the individuals and between them and their environment."[24] Repressive desublimation saps Eros; it strengthens the hold of the reality principle over Eros. Marcuse argues that a feature of repressive desublimation is a form of alienation which involves a separation of the instinctual and intellectual spheres; the individual no longer has integrated modes of thought and feeling. There is no ground on which theory and practice meet; classes no longer seem to be the basis of change. Marcuse, however, is not an advocate of the "return to the farm" school of thought. His theory of liberation is a theory for an advanced industrial society. As he notes, the break with technological rationality involves the continued existence of the technical base itself.

One-Dimensional Man does not preclude the possibility of change. Marcuse's dialectical thinking becomes obvious with his idea that the work world contains the seeds of its own destruction through the concept of stored energy. The work world becomes the potential basis for a new freedom. Qualitative change for Marcuse, however, involves much more than institutional change.

Such qualitatively new mode of existence can never be envisaged as the mere by-product of economic and political changes, as the more or less spontaneous effect of the new institutions which constitute the necessary prerequisite. Qualitative change also involves a change in the *technical* basis on which this society rests—one which sustains the economic and political institutions through the "second Nature" of man as an aggressive object of administration is stabilized. The techniques of industrialization are political techniques; as such, they prejudge the possibilities of Reason and Freedom.[25]

SUMMARY

Technology, which was to become the means to separate civilization and necessity, becomes instead the basis for a perverted Sartrian project of total administration. The lack of private space results in individuals who totally, mimetically, identify with the needs of society. Two-dimensional culture is being liquidated. Those elements, including cultural ones, which stood in opposition to the existing reality, are becoming diffused and absorbed into the one-dimensional reality. Eros is not being loosened; in effect, libido is localized and aggression rampages. However, there is still the potential for change.

With an *Essay on Liberation*, Marcuse begins to see a break in the one-dimensionality. He consciously constructs a synthesis: "In the following chapters, I attempt to develop some ideas first submitted in *Eros and Civilization* and *One-Dimensional Man*."[26] The revolutionary forces, he argues, "have taken the idea of revolution out of the continuum of repression and placed it into its authentic dimension: that of liberation."[27]

Critical theory has always been bounded by its refusal to go beyond the objective historical conditions in its attempts to find alternatives. Marcuse revises this stance and, by doing so, revises the idea of utopia. Now what is utopian becomes not that which is not possible but that which is blocked. Since Marcuse is a materialist, he believes that the potentials for liberation arise from the nature of the historical process itself. To say that the existing reality "blocks" these potentials is to say that the particular concrete historical society prevents the dialectical emergence of these negating potentialities. This history of class society has blocked the emergence of an instinctual basis for freedom. A change in the nature of man is possible because of a stage reached due to technical progress. Reality "no longer need be defined by the debilitating competition for social survival and advancement."[28] Technical progress, which seemed to destroy the revolutionary potential of the working class, still contains a possibility for liberation based on the elimination of scarcity. Since the existing class societies cannot be the agent of change because the class society produces a need for domination and suppression, the changes must be preceded by a political practice which will change the infrastructure of man, "a radical transvaluation of values."[29] This process must involve a change in man's perception, a "New Sensibility."

Marcuse links the infrastructure of man to the infrastructure of society. When he speaks of the infrastructure, he speaks of the domain of needs. He argues that the rebellion will be biological, that is, it will involve an actual change in the instinctual level. His comments on the exact nature of this biological change are minimal. They are most succinctly contained in a footnote in *An Essay on Liberation*.[30]

Marcuse introduces new categories for this revised critical analysis of society: moral, political, and aesthetic. Sexuality, when liberalized within the framework of existing society, "provides an instinctual basis for the repressive and aggressive power of affluent society."[31] The political rebellion must be a moral rebellion. Marcuse argues that the organism contains a predisposition (perhaps rooted in Eros) for morality. This disposition is Marcuse's basis for liberation, "an instinctual foundation for solidarity among human beings—a solidarity which has been effectively repressed in line with the requirements of class society but which now appears as a precondition for liberation."[32] This foundation is historical; however, human nature is malleable even in the instinctual structure, and so changes in morality can reach this level.

The first nature of man consists of the biological needs; the second nature can contain new needs. Biological needs are those for which there is no adequate substitute, and certain cultural needs can attain the status of biological needs. A biological need for freedom is possible, and this need can serve as a form for determining the individual's perception.

Science and technology are the vehicles of liberation, and it is only the form in which they are used which links them to domination. This fact is what enables *An Essay on Liberation* to follow *One-Dimensional Man:* the advancements of modern technological society of and by themselves do not preclude the development of a non-repressive society. These advances are vital for liberation. Without them, society would be forced to maintain a level of repression commensurate with scarcity. It is one of Marcuse's fundamental tenets that scarcity per se has been overcome as a limiting factor for the human condition.

Objectively, the laboring class is still the revolutionary class; subjectively, it is not. This is another important advance from *One-Dimensional Man.* Marcuse argues that the idea of a new man can be found in Marx and Engels but only as a member and not a builder of the new society. The new subverting forces may signal the formation of a new revolutionary basis, "the new historical

Subject of change, responding to the new objective conditions with qualitatively different needs and aspirations."[33] A shift toward subjective factors is a characteristic of these subverting forces. A radical change in consciousness "is the beginning, the first step in changing social existence: emergence of the new Subject."[34]

A new reality principle would emerge under which a new aesthetic ethos would be created. Under this new aesthetic ethos, individuals would be free from the guilt of their ancestors. The aesthetic, the third new category for the critical analysis of society, is the possible form of the new society. The "aesthetic truth" had been monopolized by the higher culture; but, because of the spread of mass culture, it has been liberated. The dialectic has triumphed. Marcuse searches for something in the idea of the aesthetic which contains the potential for freedom in its new form. He draws his concept of an aesthetic dimension from Schiller, a Kantian dualist. According to Marcuse, Schiller's work contains the image of a nonrepressive reality. A brief summary of Schiller's major points is in order, for Marcuse basically uncritically accepts Schiller in regard to these formulations. For Schiller, man can make his way to Freedom through Beauty; he must approach the problem of politics through the problem of the aesthetic.

Schiller identifies two drives in man: the sensuous and the formal. The sensuous drive, based in man's physical existence, sets man within the limits of time and turns him into matter. For Schiller, matter is reality which occupies time. This drive, known as sensation, gives man his determinate existence, for without time (without becoming), man exists only as potential.

The formal drive proceeds from man's rational nature. It affirms his Person among all the changes of Condition, that is, instead of man being in time, time is in man. This drive affirms man as a species-being. Schiller conceives of man as Person (formal drive) and Person in a particular Condition (sensuous drive). Change and becoming correspond to man as Person in a particular Condition, and species and unity correspond to Person. "Only inasmuch as he changes does he exist; only inasmuch as he remains unchangeable does he exist."[35]

It appears man must forever exist as unfulfilled. How can he both participate in time and remain above time? How can he both participate in change and remain a constant unity? The drives appear to be diametrically opposed. But, as Schiller elaborates, this is not so. The sensuous drive does not demand change in Person; the formal drive does not insist on unity or persistence in Condition.

The sense drive needs the form drive, and the form drive needs the sense drive. If the sense drive dominates, the world becomes a force rather than an object; and man becomes only a content of time and has no content, no existence himself. If the form drive overcomes feeling and the Person takes the place of the world, Person takes the place of the object and ceases to be an autonomous force and subject. Absolute reality needs limitation.

Schiller describes a third drive in which the sense and form drives act in concert. This is the play drive, which has as its object living form, all the aesthetic qualities of phenomena. The play drive sets man physically and morally free by annulling all contingency and all constraint. In the contemplation of the beautiful, the psyche is in an area between the realm of law and the sphere of physical exigency, removed from the constraint of both.

Freedom can arise only when man is a complete being with both drives fully developed. Play makes him whole and unfolds both sides of his nature at once. Beauty links the opposite conditions of feeling and thinking.

Sensation precedes consciousness and so the sense drive precedes the form drive. Man cannot pass directly into thought from feeling; he has to pass through a middle disposition in which sense and reason are active at the same time. This middle disposition is the aesthetic. In the aesthetic dimension, man emancipates himself from the subjugation of nature and passes through to the moral, where he becomes the master of nature. In the first state man is autistic; he is but a passive recipient of the sensory world. His development of contemplation initiates his step toward culture. His development proceeds to an interest in semblance and away from the strictures of reality.

For Marcuse, Beauty as desired object speaks of the domain of Eros and Thanatos. Marcuse finds in the history of the discussion of the aesthetic a focus on the idea of the beautiful which expresses "the aesthetic *ethos* which provides the common denominator of the aesthetic and the political."[36] It is these qualities which enable the aesthetic dimension to "serve as a sort of gauge for a free society."[37] The aesthetic needs have a social content which is counter to the fulfillment of needs in the existing society. The imagination depends upon the senses and upon reason. The senses provide the material, the data which can then be transformed by imagination.

> The freedom of the imagination is thus restrained by the order of sensibility, not only by its pure forms (space and time), but also by its empirical content, which, as the object-world to be transcended, remains a determining factor in the transcendence.[38]

The freedom of imagination depends also on reason for conceptual mastery and interpretation. The political protest can, in effect, politicize the apolitical aesthetic dimension, activating a fundamental human sensibility and rebelliousness. The imagination could radically reconstruct experience after it has been freed from its link to exploitation.

The collapse of the segregated sphere of higher values is one of the fundamental causes of this potential for liberation. This segregated sphere had contained the aesthetic truth-power. The reintegrative power that was spoken about in *Eros and Civilization* as therapeutic was set up to be freed by the apparently repressive desublimation of *One-Dimensional Man*. Art could then become "a productive force in the material as well as cultural transformation."[39] Marcuse claims that this will actually be the "end" of art as the ascent of Form—pure forms other than Kant's space and time.

For Marcuse, the new language indicates the "depth of the rebellion."[40] The new sensibility is united with the new rationality. However, this change in consciousness among certain groups must be spread; there must be a "period of enlightenment prior to material change," education which turns into praxis.[41] The radicalization of the objective revolutionary class will depend upon "catalysts outside its ranks."[42]

During the 1960s, Marcuse achieved a position unusual for a contemporary political philosopher; he became the apologist for a generation of people concerned with social change. Since then, both interest in Marcuse and participation in direct political actions have significantly declined. Marcuse's writings themselves provide ample work for students of political philosophy. However, it is the direction in which Marcuse can lead political philosophy that merits, even demands, consideration; and this will be the subject of the remainder of this study.

NOTES

1. Martin Jay, *The Dialectical Imagination* (Boston: Little, Brown and Company, 1973).

2. Kurt H. Wolff and Barrington Moore, Jr., eds., *The Critical Spirit* (Boston: Beacon Press, 1967); Sidney Lipshires, *Herbert Marcuse: From Marx to Freud and Beyond* (Cambridge, Mass.: Schenkman Publishing Company, 1974).

3. The following articles provide a cursory understanding of Marcuse's thought as well as a conception of his image in the popular press: L. Abel, "Seven Heroes of the New Left," *New York Times Magazine,* May 5, 1968, pp. 30-31; E. Andrew, "Work and Freedom in Marcuse and Marx," *Canadian Journal of Political Science* 3 (June 1970), pp. 241-56; W. Leiss, "Reply with Rejoinder to E. Andrew," *Canadian Journal of Political Science* 4 (September 1971), pp. 398-404; J. Burnham, "Sock It to Us, Herbert," *National Review,* November 19, 1968, p. 1158; D. Callahan, "Resistance and Technology," *Commonweal,* December 22, 1967, pp. 377-81; D. Sullivan, "Reply with Rejoinder to Callahan," *Commonweal,* December 22, 1967, pp. 377-81; E. Capouya, "What We Don't Know Might Kill Us," *Saturday Review,* March 28, 1964, pp. 26-27; P. Clecak, "Marcuse: Ferment of Hope," *Nation,* June 16, 1969, pp. 765-68; P. Delany, "Marcuse in the Seventies," *Partisan Review,* 40, No. 3 (1973), pp. 455-60; Paul Eidelberg, "The Temptation of Herbert Marcuse," *Review of Politics* 31 (October 1969), pp. 442-58; John Fremstad, "Marcuse: The Dialectics of Hopelessness," *Western Political Quarterly* 30 (March 1977), pp. 80-92; Sam B. Girgus, "Howells and Marcuse: A Forecast of the One-Dimensional Age," *American Quarterly* 25 (March 1973), pp. 108-18; K. Glaser, "Marcuse and the German New Left," *National Review,* July 2, 1968, p. 649; H. Gold, "California Left: Mao, Marx, et Marcuse." *Saturday Evening Post,* October 19, 1968, pp. 56-59; Lucien Goldman, "Understanding Marcuse," *Partisan Review,* No. 3 (1971), pp. 247-62; Herbert Marcuse, "A Reply to Lucien Goldman," *Partisan Review* (Winter 1971-72), pp. 397-400; R. Goodwin, "Social Theory of Herbert Marcuse," *Atlantic* (June 1971), pp. 68-70; Richard Greeman, "A Critical Re-Examination of Herbert Marcuse's Works," *New*

Politics (Fall 1967), pp. 12-23; J. Groutt, "Marcuse and Goodwin Tangle at
Temple," *Commonweal*, May 23, 1969, pp. 279-80; R. Hindery, "Marcuse's Eroticized Man," *Christian Century*, February 4, 1970, pp. 136-38;
G. Kateb, "Political Thought of Herbert Marcuse," *Commentary* (January
1970), pp. 48-63; "Legion vs. Marcuse," *Nation*, October 28, 1968, p.
421; J.W. Montgomery, "Marcuse," *Christianity Today*, April 24, 1970,
p. 47; M. Peretz. "Herbert Marcuse: Beyond Technological Reason," *Yale
Review* 57 (June 1968), pp. 518-27; M. Schoolman, "Further Reflections
on Work, Alienation, and Freedom in Marcuse and Marx," *Canadian
Journal of Political Science* 6 (June 1973), pp. 295-302; Ian Slater, "Orwell,
Marcuse, and the Language of Politics," *Political Studies* 23 (December
1975), pp. 459-74; M.J. Sobran, "Future Future of Marcuse," *National
Review*, December 8, 1972, p. 1352; David Spitz, "Pure Tolerance,"
Dissent (September-October 1966), pp. 510-25; S. Stern, "Metaphysics
of Rebellion," *Ramparts*, June 29, 1968, pp. 55-60; E. Stillman, "Marcuse,"
Horizon (Summer 1969), pp. 26-31; "Camus and Some Others," *Times
Literary Supplement*, January 29, 1970, pp. 97-98; J.K. Walsh, "Why
Marcuse Matters," *Commonweal*, October 2, 1970, pp. 21-25; P. Walton,
"From Surplus Value to Surplus Theories: Marx, Marcuse, and MacIntyre,"
Social Research 37 (December 1970), pp. 644-55; Jerzy J. Wiatr, "Herbert
Marcuse: Philosopher of a Lost Radicalism," trans. H.F. Mins, *Science
and Society* 34 (Fall 1970), pp. 319-30; Anthony Wilden, "Marcuse and
the Freudian Model: Energy, Information, and Phantasie," *Salmagundi*
(Fall 1969-Winter 1970), pp. 196-245; I.A. Zamoshkin and N.V. Motroshilova, "Is Marcuse's Critical Theory of Society Critical?" *Soviet Review*
11 (Spring 1970), pp. 3-24; and Y. Zhukov, "Taking Marcuse to the
Woodshed," *Atlas* (September 1968), pp. 33-35. Marcuse's major studies
have been reviewed within a number of disciplines, which is an indication
of the scope of both his interests and the interest surrounding his work:
"Soviet Marxism: A Critical Analysis," *Review of Political Studies* 7 (June
1959), pp. 181-83; Kurt H. Wolff, review of *Eros and Civilization*, by
Herbert Marcuse, in *American Journal of Sociology* 62 (November 1956),
pp. 342-43; Abraham Edel, "Instead of Repression," review of *Eros and
Civilization*, by Herbert Marcuse, in *Nation*, July 7, 1956, p. 22; H. Finga-
rette, review of *Eros and Civilization*, by Herbert Marcuse, in *Review
of Metaphysics* 10 (June 1957), pp. 660-65; I. Howe, "Herbert Marcuse or
Milovan Djilas," review of *Eros and Civilization*, by Herbert Marcuse, in
Harper's (July 1969), p. 84; D. Braybrooke, "Marcuse's Merits," review of
An Essay on Liberation and Negations, by Herbert Marcuse, in *Trans-
Action* (October 1969), pp. 51-54; J. Sparrow, "Marcuse: The Gospel of
Hate," review of *An Essay on Liberation*, by Herbert Marcuse, in *National*

Review, October 21, 1969, pp. 1068-69; K. Widmer, "Society as a Work of Art," review of *Five Lectures*, by Herbert Marcuse, in *Nation*, July 6, 1970, p. 211; and R.A. Krieger, "Latest Dispatch from the Barricades," review of *Counterrevolution and Revolt*, by Herbert Marcuse, in *Business Week*, June 17, 1972, p. 12. Marcuse himself, during the student revolt of the 1960s, became the subject of many articles. The tenor of these articles can be suggested by a brief examination of the following pieces: Eliseo Vivas, "Incoherent Nihilist," *National Review*, July 14, 1970, p. 739; I Kristol, "Improbable Guru of Surrealistic Politics," *Fortune* (July 1969), p. 191; M. Cohen, "Norman Vincent Peale of the Left," *Atlantic* (June 1969), p. 108; and "One-Dimensional Philosopher," *Time*, March 22, 1968, p. 38. The following books deal exclusively with Marcuse or include him in a discussion of more general subjects: Robert W. Marks, *The Meaning of Marcuse* (New York: Ballantine Books, 1970); Eliseo Vivas, *Contra Marcuse* (New York: Dell Publishing Co., A Delta Book, 1971); Alasdair MacIntyre, *Herbert Marcuse: An Exposition and a Polemic* (New York: Viking Press, Modern Masters, 1970); Maurice Cranston, ed., *The New Left* (New York: Library Press, 1971), p. 116; Paul A. Robinson, *The Freudian Left* (New York: Harper and Row, 1969); Paul Breines, ed., *Critical Interruptions* (New York: Herder and Herder, Inc., 1970); Gad Horowitz, *Repression* (Toronto: University of Toronto Press, 1977); Richard King, *The Party of Eros* (Chapel Hill: University of North Carolina Press, 1972); Irving Howe, ed., *Beyond the New Left* (New York: McCall Publishing Company, 1970); John P. Diggins, *The American Left in the Twentieth Century* (New York: Harcourt Brace Jovanovich, Inc., 1973); and Jack Woddis, *New Theories of Revolution* (New York: International Publishers, 1972). Marcuse has also been the subject of dissertations, for example: Allen Yehuda Graubard, "The Political Position of Herbert Marcuse" (unpublished Ph. D. dissertation, Harvard, 1970); Francis Joseph McVeigh, "Comparative Analysis of Ortega y Gasset's and Herbert Marcuse's Theories of Social Change" (Ph. D. diss. St. John's University, 1970). The following dissertations are either still in progress or, if completed, have not been placed on film in the Library of Congress: David Bethune, "The Political Philosophy of Herbert Marcuse" (Ph.D. diss. in progress, Tulane University, 1971); Gordon A. Hunter, "Herbert Marcuse: A Critical Examination of His Political Teaching" (Ph.D. diss. in progress, University of Chicago, 1969); and Lawrence M. Shapiro, "The Neo-Marxism of Herbert Marcuse" (Ph.D. diss. in progress, Columbia University, 1971).

    4. Theodore Roszak, *The Making of a Counter Culture* (Garden City, N.Y.: Doubleday and Company, Inc., 1969).

5. Ibid., p. 91.

6. Ibid., p. 93.

7. Ibid., p. 95.

8. Cranston, ed., *The New Left*, pp. 92-93.

9. Ibid., p. 114.

10. Robinson, *The Freudian Left*, p. 201.

11. For an interesting discussion of the importance of the distinction between basic and surplus repression, see Horowitz, *Repression*. Horowitz responds to critics of Marcuse, such as Lipshires, who overlook the importance of this distinction.

12. B. Parekh, "Utopianism and Manicheism: A Critique of Marcuse's Theory of Revolution," *Social Research* 39 (Winter 1972), p. 64.

13. Herbert Marcuse, "A Reply to Lucien Goldman," *Partisan Review* (Winter, 1971-72), pp. 398-99.

14. Ibid., p. 399.

15. Parekh, "Utopianism and Manicheism," p. 650.

16. Herbert Marcuse, *An Essay on Liberation* (Boston: Beacon Press, 1969), p. 25.

17. Herbert Marcuse, *Eros and Civilization* (New York: Random House, 1955, Vintage Books Edition, 1972), p. 39.

18. Ibid., p. 41.

19. Ibid., p. 94.

20. Ibid., p. 95.

21. Herbert Marcuse, *One-Dimensional Man* (Boston: Beacon Press, 1964), p. 10.

22. Ibid.

23. Ibid., p. 84.

24. Marcuse, *Eros and Civilization*, p. *ix*.

25. Marcuse, *One-Dimensional Man*, p. 18.

26. Marcuse, *An Essay on Liberation*, p. *ix*.

27. Ibid., p. *x*.

28. Ibid., p. 5.

29. Ibid., p. 6.

30. I use the terms *biological* and *biology* not in the sense of the scientific discipline, but in order to designate the processes and the dimension in which inclinations, behavior patterns, and aspirations become vital needs which, if not satisfied, would cause dysfunction of the organism. Conversely, socially induced needs and aspirations may result in a more pleasurable organic behavior. If biological needs are defined as those which must be satisfied and for which no adequate substitute can be provided, certain cultural needs can "sink down" into the biology of man. We could

then speak, for example, of the biological need of freedom, or of some aesthetic needs as having taken root in the organic structure of man, in his "nature" or, rather, in his "second nature." This usage of the term *biological* does not imply or assume anything as to the way in which needs are physiologically expressed and transmitted (Marcuse, *An Essay on Liberation*, p. 10).

31. Ibid., p. 9.

32. Ibid., p. 10.

33. Ibid., p. 52.

34. Ibid., p. 53.

35. Friedrich Schiller, *On the Aesthetic Education of Man—In a Series of Letters* (1795), ed. and trans, Elizabeth M. Wilkinson and L.A. Willoughby (Oxford: Clarendon Press, 1967), p. 75.

36. Ibid., p. 26.

37. Ibid., p. 27.

38. Ibid., p. 29.

39. Ibid., p. 32.

40. Ibid., p. 36.

41. Ibid., p. 53.

42. Ibid., p. 54.

CHAPTER 3

Marcuse in Depth: A More Detailed Examination of His Vision

Marcuse's therapeutic vision, like his dialectical logic, is firmly rooted in the human condition; his symbolic conception of the ordering nature of the political is not an illusory attempt to impose a veneer of rationality on human existence. This chapter has a dual purpose: it locates some of the elements of his therapeutic vision in terms of the tradition of political discourse, and it develops in greater detail the critical components of that vision.

Philosophy, for Marcuse, must maintain a critical tension between the real and the potential. This necessity provides a key to an understanding of Marcuse's admiration for Hegel and his rejection of the British empiricists.

According to Marcuse, it is man's capacity as a thinking being which enables him to order rather than merely receive his reality; and it is reason which can oppose the existing reality. The French Revolution, for Hegel, demonstrated reason's power over reality.[1] Only man, in Hegel's system, has an understanding of potentialities; only man is a self-determining subject. Existence becomes a process of actualizing potentialities according to reason. Hegel, like Marcuse, links reason and freedom:

Reason presupposes freedom, the power to act in accordance with knowledge of the truth, the power to shape reality in line with its potentialities. The fulfillment of these ends belongs only to the subject who is master of his own development and who understands his own potentialities as well as those of the things around him. Freedom, in turn, presupposes reason, for it is comprehending knowledge, alone, that enables the subject to gain and wield this power.[2]

Marcuse is critical of idealism which, in his terms, would forget the "miserable social world" and speak instead of "the refuge for truth, goodness, beauty, happiness, and, most important, for a critical temper which could not be turned into social channels."[3] Marcuse argues that although Hegel was in this tradition of idealism, the latter's critical impulse was powerful enough to make him aware of historical reality. Hegel, says Marcuse, "made philosophy a concrete historical factor and drew history into philosophy."[4]

In effect, the German idealists were responding to the British empiricists' argument that it is habit, not reason, which "adheres" to but never "governs" facts (sense experience). For the idealists, the failure to ground this active, ordering role would result in the victimization of the species; that is, man would be left ineffectual against unknowable and unmasterable social forces of material existence.

Marcuse sees in idealism a conception of reason which allows the individual to go beyond what is to what ought to be. Idealist universality provides the opportunity for transcendence. In contrast, Marcuse argues that the British empiricists restricted knowledge to the given, thereby effectively destroying transcendence and resulting in despair of and about what is.

Marcuse also admires Hegel for recognizing that full existence can come only in social life, that the liberation of the individual is linked to the liberation of society. Marx, as Marcuse reads him, employs these same idealist conceptions. For Marx, man is a species-being because he treats himself as a universal and therefore free being. Therefore, freedom for Marx is linked to man's ability to act, to relate to his own species. Man must appropriate the object world. Marx identifies objective being with sensuous being. For Marx, to be sensuous is to be passive.

But in Marx it is this concept of sensuousness (as objectification) which leads to the decisive turn from classical German philosophy to the theory of revolution, for he inserts the basic traits of *practical* and *social* existence into his definition of man's essential being. As objectivity, man's sensuous-

ness is essentially practical objectification, and because it is practical it is
essentially a social objectification.[5]

Man can transcend what is, appropriate it, give it to his own reality, and realize himself. Man's "life-activity" is "free activity"; he
can produce himself and his objectivity.[6] Society, for Marx, is not
above the individual; the individual is a social being.

In effect, Marcuse also attacks existentialism for its rejection of
universals, which he believes resulted in the rejection of universally
valid rational norms for society and state. The existentialists argued that there were no bonds joining individuals into a community and that reason cannot be the judge for individual existential experience. They believed that "Laws . . . are not based
upon any universal qualities of man in whom a reason resides; they
rather express the needs of individual people whose lives they
regulate in accordance with their existential requirements."[7] Ironically, Marcuse links the existentialists and not Hegel with fascism:
"This demotion of reason made it possible to exalt certain par-
ticularities (such as the race or the folk) to the rank of the highest
values."[8]

Marcuse sees existentialism as a response to a perceived absurdity
of the world, a reality which appears to refute rationalism. For
Cartesian philosophy the reality is in the self, but for existentialism
there is no rational universe. In the absurd world, death and time
are denials of meaning. It is man, for existentialism, who must
accept the challenge of finding his own freedom and happiness.

Sartre clearly puzzles Marcuse, for he sees strains in Sartre's
writing which link him to Marxism as well as ideas which place him
in contradiction to Marx. For Marcuse, Sartre's conceptions are
metaphysical and metahistorical; that is, he sees Sartre's theory as
separate from any historical reality. Freedom for Sartre is the
human being itself, and man is fully responsible for his own being.
His situation is his insofar as he engages in it. His being is his action,
his self-creation. Marcuse denies that everyone has his own absolute free choice. For Sartre, revolution presupposes the freedom to
seize revolution; this, for Sartre, destroys the materialist idea that
man is determined by the material world. Marcuse argues that
Marx is aware of the importance of the maturity of revolutionary
consciousness:

Marx's constant emphasis on the material determination of the consciousness in all its manifestations points up the relationships between the subject and his world as they actually prevail in the capitalist society, where freedom has shrunk to the possibility of recognizing and seizing the necessity for liberation.[9]

Marcuse appears to be arguing that this absolute material determination of consciousness is not an inevitability, that the Great Refusal is a critical break in this relationship between material existence and consciousness. Marcuse, it is possible to conclude, never abandons Hegel.

The critical element of idealist philosophy (to which Marcuse remains ever loyal) was that all that was not reasonable was that which had to be overcome. The world, for idealist philosophy, was susceptible to the structure of reason. Reason was the fundamental category of thought and corresponded to the highest potentiality. Being was subsumed under thought. For bourgeois philosophy, however, reason takes the form of rational subjectivity. Reason contains freedom; to submit to reason would be meaningless without the capacity to act on the attained judgment. Marcuse argues that with this concept of reason as freedom, philosophy seemed to reach its limit. Kant, according to Marcuse, leaves us with the conclusion that factual transformation was unnecessary; since reason was transcendent, "individuals could become rational and free within the established order."[10] This internalization of idealism leads, following Marcuse, to the illusion of freedom and reason rather than true freedom and reason. As Marcuse notes, "Reason and freedom become tasks that the individual is to fulfill within himself, and he can do so regardless of external conditions."[11] In idealism, the individual makes himself and the world free in thought. Reason should create a "universality and community" in which rational subjects participate.[12] Marcuse argues that bourgeois philosophy results in this illusion of freedom. He calls for a cancellation of the restriction of reason to pure thought and will. He would equate the demand for reason with the demand for the creation of a rational social organization, that is, an external reality erected in accordance with true human needs.

For critical theory, the goals come from tendencies of the social process.

Therefore it has no fear of the utopia that the new order is denounced as being. When truth cannot be realized within the established social order, it always appears to the latter as mere utopia. This transcendence speaks not against, but for, its truth. The utopian element was long the only progressive element in philosophy, as in the constructions of the best state and the highest pleasure, of perfect happiness and perpetual peace. The obstinacy that comes from adhering to truth against all appearances has given way in contemporary philosophy to whimsy and uninhibited opportunism. Critical theory preserves obstinacy as a genuine quality of philosophic thought.[13]

Marcuse's vision is materialist because it is grounded in what he regards as the materialist process of fantasy. Critical theory, like philsophy, holds that man can be more than the subject in the production process. Materialist critical theory argues that man should not confine his demands to a transcendent realm. Marcuse condemns Aristotle and Kant for what he considers to be the degradation of fantasy. For Marcuse, conceptual thought is insufficient to rationalize reality. As he notes, "In order to retain what is not yet present as a goal in the present phantasy is required."[14] Philosophical knowledge, without fantasy, "remains in the grip of the present or the past and severed from the future, which is the only link between philosophy and the real history of mankind."[15] Fantasy, Marcuse would argue, has the potential of future-directed power. Aristotle and Kant would diffuse this power of fantasy by labeling it "imagination" and restricting it to a priori tasks. Marcuse speaks of fantasy in terms of man's relation to symbols. Critical theory, which does not deny the power of fantasy, can bring to consciousness potentialities which emerge within the developing reality.

Marcuse's philosophic vision would engage the reality of concrete existence in a therapeutic attempt to infuse liberating alternatives into one-dimensional society. He attacks theories which deny the ordering and transcending power of reason. For Marcuse, it is sensuous reason which will oppose total administration. Bourgeois philosophy, in effect, fails to deal with the totality of human existence and is therefore ineffectual in providing opposition to what is. Conceptual thought is insufficient to rationalize reality; in other words, that which deals only with the conscious dimension of existence cannot order the world in accordance with what Marcuse considers to be true human needs. The political philosopher must tap another dimension of human existence to give his vision therapeutic power. This insight is Marcuse's most important contribution to the recognition, expansion, and development of the therapeutic function of political philosophy. Marcuse's efforts, however, are not totally successful. In fact, his pessimism can often be traced to the ineffectuality of his symbolic conceptualizations. However, such an argument is premature. It is mandatory to lay a foundation for the incorporation of symbolic and mythical elements into political philosophy before proceeding to a more complex discussion of the proper conception of the nature and function of these elements and their relationship to the therapeutic function of the political philosopher's vision.

Deutsch argues that "theory" has an objective and a subjective meaning. The objective meaning of theory regards the ability "to see and perceive something outside the observing self, even though the object of the observation may be within one's own larger personality."[16] The subjective meaning relates to the ability "to perceive this object as relevant to one's own emotions, needs, or desires"; and it is this meaning which necessitates the use of symbolic and mythical language in the discussion of what is political and what constitutes the function of the political vision.[17]

This need has been spoken to by McDonald, who links politics and myth. It is myth, McDonald argues, which can help to transform and to link old and new. Myths have universality and are bearers of meanings beyond the given. McDonald's argument is based upon a distinction he makes between "data" and "danda." McDonald, following Stephen Pepper, distinguishes data, "evidence refined through multiplicative corroboration, by repetitive tests, or by observations of a similar kind made by a series of observers," from danda, "evidence refined through structural corroboration by measuring conformity to a preexisting construct."[18] For McDonald, if science is only data collection, then mythical elements have no place in the language of political science; but, "If science means also explanation and elucidation by the structural corroboration of danda," then there is room in the language of even political science for mythical elements.[19] Even

Easton, McDonald argues, builds his system on "analogy, metaphor, and possibly myth."[20]

Concerning the role of symbolism in political thought, Michael Walzer writes that "politics is the art of unification; from many, it makes one. And symbolic activity is perhaps our most important means of bringing things together, both intellectually and emotionally, thus overcoming isolation and even individuality."[21]

It then appears that this incorporation of symbolic and mythical elements into the language of political discourse is a necessary step in the search for ideas which will speak to the totality of human existence. The need to include this element of man's experience in the tradition of political discourse has been noted by Zashin and Chapman and by Edelman.

In their article on the use of metaphor and analogy, Zashin and Chapman urge the adoption of a political language that will make the reality of our time comprehensible. They argue that theorists in the tradition of political discourse used a language that was rich enough to speak to all people, not only an isolated academic group. They urge that such a language, which would include the use of metaphor, analogy, and symbol, be adopted in the discussion of the political.

A more general crisis of integration is developing: the various institutional domains of society are becoming more opaque to those outside them and even to those playing subordinate roles within them. The totality is beyond the comprehension of most individuals and no unifying meaning system *intelligible to the great mass of the population* is available to legitimate the society seen as a system.[22]

Edelman, too, emphasizes this need to include symbols in the tradition of political discourse (his thoughts can also be extended to the possible pathological effects of symbolic gratification, an issue which will be considered in a later chapter). For Edelman, "the symbolic side of politics calls for attention, for men cannot know themselves until they know what they do and what surrounds and nurtures them."[23] The study of symbols enables us to reach a better understanding of man before he comes to terms with specifics of his sociohistorical reality.

What Eliade calls the "non-historical reality" contains memories of a more complete existence.[24] Highly civilized individuals may be unable to find access to symbols, for symbols must be approached by an integrated being.

> An a uniter of opposites the symbol is a totality which can never be addressed only to one faculty in man—his reason or intellect, for example —but always concerns our wholeness, touches and produces a resonance in all four of our functions at once. The symbol as "image" has the character of a summons and stimulates a man's whole being to a total reaction; his thought and feeling, his senses and his intuition participate in this reaction and it is not, as some mistakenly suppose, a single one of his functions that is actualized.[25]

Marcuse's diagnosis of contemporary society includes a perception of most individuals as being among those who are "highly civilized" and therefore incapable of directly finding access to symbols. This access-creating function, for Marcuse, becomes the function of the political philosopher and his vision.

Marcuse attempts to demonstrate the potential for a new reality principle through the use of symbols validated in the aesthetic dimension. Marcuse is conscious of the relationship between symbols and existence and is, in effect, with his images of Orpheus and Narcissus, self-consciously attempting to discuss symbols and to meet the demands of a new reality no longer characterized by scarcity.

MARCUSE'S VISION AS A SYMBOLIC ORDERING

Marcuse's vision involves the removal of man from the historical realm of necessity. In effect, he proposes to negate time as that which binds man to repression and domination.

Following Glass, it is possible to argue that Marcuse's philosophic vision is one of harmonia: "For political philosophers, however, concept or thought allows man to transcend his aggressive patterns; philosophy, given the opportunity and the timing, possesses the power to remake human nature, to heal societies wounded through the operation of historical processes."[26] The philosopher, like the shaman, aids the individual in the transformation of consciousness from profane time to sacred time, from the determining aspects of time to time as meaningless, from becoming to being. This same denial of the destructiveness of time, history, and necessity is present in the philosophic vision. The vision attempts to generate, from the unconscious, an erotic vision of unity. Consciousness is liberated "from domination by the 'profane' world" and is rendered "receptive to dynamic and vitalized symbols."[27] It is this energy which can "heal" the destructiveness and separatedness of the historical process. What "dies" is our historical self. The reality of the historical world is corrupt, and "The vision implies a denunciation of a corrupt reality and the embracing of alternative signs having no connection with specific historical interests."[28]

Philosophy has a force which can break through corrupt historical realities and transform the perceived historical nature of man through an unconscious unity.

Like the shaman, if the philosopher can show that the causes of suffering exist as alien intrusions in the "true" human and political constitution, if pain exists as an unnatural perversion of what "can be" (a condition of health), then the argument may become persuasive in the consciousness of an audience.[29]

Political philosophy in its therapeutic function attempts to lift man out of the realm of what Eliade calls profane time and into the realm of sacred time. The therapeutic tool of the political philosopher is his vision, a response to the disease of man which is linked to the idea of the destructiveness of history and time. The realm of society is the realm of time, of necessity. It was the notion of the political as opposed to this realm of necessity that gave the self substance outside of this historical determinism. Time appears as the critical element to be reckoned with, the main element with which philosophy must contend.

Eliade distinguishes sacred time from its opposite, profane time. The sacred is not an isolated realm but, like the profane, a mode of being in the world in which there is a conception of time and space as not homogeneous. Sacred space and sacred time are the "real" space and time. For Eliade, every myth has as its paradigm the cosmogonic myth. Sacred time is reversible. "It [sacred time] is an ontological, Parmenidean time; it always remains equal to itself, it neither changes nor is exhausted."[30]

The conception of sacred time has therapeutic implications, for

What is involved is, in short, a return to the original time, the therapeutic purpose of which to to begin life once again, a symbolic rebirth. The conception underlying these curative rituals seems to be the following: life cannot be repaired, it can only be recreated through symbolic repetition of the cosmogony, for, as we have said, the cosmogony is the paradigmatic model for all creation.[31]

Eliade argues that while primitive religious man is concerned with sacred history, modern nonreligious man sees himself only in terms of profane history, as the subject and agent of history. Modern man rejects transcendence and any model for humanity which is not a part of the human condition. Eliade argues that there is no such thing as a purely rational man. Man, for Eliade, is composed of conscious and unconscious; and it is in the unconscious that what Eliade calls the religious idea remains, an idea which could provide a transcendent model for man in the idea of the sacred.

Eliade conceives of myth as an expression of a "mode of being in the world."[32] He argues that myths remain a part of human experience and are manifest in dreams and fantasies. Eliade relates modern man's anxiety to an attempt to deny this type of reality. He contends that modern man has a passion for what he calls "historiography," a desire for knowledge of the past of humanity. Eliade links this passion for historiography to modern man's anxiety, particularly in relation to death. For modern man, death is nothingness. Death in non-European cultures is not viewed as nothingness but as a passing to another mode of being, manifesting itself in symbols of resurrection or rebirth. The anguish of the primitive man concerning death is the anguish of initiation. The symbolism of death is linked to the symbolism of regeneration. Death represents a passage from profane time, a rebirth.

A passage in R.D. Laing's *Politics of Experience* is analogous to the process undergone by Eliade's primitive man:

When a person goes mad, a profound transposition of his place in relation to all domains of being occurs. His center of experience moves from ego to self. Mundane time becomes merely anecdotal, only the eternal matters. The madman is, however, confused. He muddles ego with self, inner with outer, natural and supernatural. Nevertheless, he can often be to us, even through his profound wretchedness and disintegration, the hierophant of the sacred. An exile from the scene of being as we know it, he is an alien, a stranger signaling to us from the void in which he is foundering, a void which may be peopled by presences that we do not even dream of.[33]

In Eliade's terms, Laing's "madman" is leaving the realm of profane time and entering the realm of sacred time. He is leaving the homogeneity of profane time and space for the discontinuity of sacred time and space. Laing, like Eliade, argues that this journey may be a therapeutic event, a process of regeneration and rebirth. The Laingian journey symbolizes what for Eliade was a reenactment of the paradigmatic model, a reenactment of the cosmogonic process on the ontogenetic level.

Laing himself notes that what he calls "transcendental experience" might be the "original wellspring of all religions."[34] Profane time becomes egoic experience, which is predicated on this homogeneity of time and space.

Most people most of the time experience themselves and others in one or another way that I shall call egoic. That is, centrally or peripherally, they experience the world and themselves in terms of a consistent identity, a me-here over against a you-there, within a framework of certain ground structures of space and time shared with other members of their society.[35]

The therapeutic function of political philosophy is premised upon a conception of the political which regards the self as possessing substance outside of the realm of society. Gunnell argues that the tradition of political thought was left a legacy, traceable to Plato, characterized by the tension between political order and history. Political order became, for Plato and Aristotle, a product of human action. For Plato, according to Gunnell, the vision was positive; the state would lift the individual and the political order out of history. Aristotle, according to Gunnell, came to regard time as a destructive force. For much of political philosophy from Plato to Rousseau, the political was set in opposition to society; the political represented order as opposed to society which was "the realm of anxiety, instability, uniqueness, the arena of passions, and the root of human disorder."[36] There were some exceptions, particularly Hobbes, who viewed man as caught "in the flux of time and overwhelmed by the instability of human affairs."[37] After Rousseau, as Gunnell interprets it, the idea of the political as a symbolic means to order chaos began to decline. This change came about because the self became linked to society, to the realm of necessity. Gunnell labels this the "historization of the human being." History and society not the transcendent political, became man's home. Before Locke, man the actor was manifest in the transcendent realm of the political which allowed him to order his existence. The problem of time which came with the development of self was resolved by defining the self in terms of the actor who, by utilizing his natural function of symbol creator, could construct a realm in which he could master time. With Locke, however, the self lost its element of transcendence.

The idea of the political had hitherto been fundamentally grounded in the assumption that a political space could be erected within the world which would conform to the nature of man, but with Locke man was known in terms of a self which was becoming little more than a floating consciousness; personal identity was simply a state of mind or a changing configuration of ideas preserved in memory.[38]

To complete this decline of the political, Marx inverted the traditional relationship between society and the political order and, Gunnell contends, "completed the foundation for the modern conceptualization of human affairs in terms of history and society."[39]

The symbolic conception of the political retains an element of the mythic; it retains a desire to annul history and in effect attain the "eternal present." Primitive man denied change and became master; Western man named change "time" and became master.

The political order becomes analogous to the creation of the cosmos; the political becomes that which allows man to become master of change, to comprehend and control the chaos by means of a created political order. Man's creation of the political is a cosmogonic event; political order represents man's attempt to recapitulate the process of creation. Political becomes synonymous with rebirth and regeneration.

For Gunnell, the mythic mode was atemporal. With the breakdown of this mode of existence, man became conscious of time and self. The mythic timelessness and selflessness were linked to a static social order; and their loss was "bound to the loss, or the threat of the loss, of an ordered social space."[40]

As man progresses out of the archetypal existence under the cosmogonic myth, time becomes a problem. A distance is created between the individual and the natural flow of events which results in the conception of self isolated from this natural flux. The individual needs something to replace the cosmological myth as that which relates him to the totality of his perceived existence. This role, for Gunnell, becomes the function of the political. Man, as a symbolic animal, creates the political as that which can integrate cosmos and society and lift man out of time.

Marcuse's vision of a non-repressive reality contains the idea of a leap from historical necessity to a realm of internal and external harmony. Marcuse, like those other thinkers who employ a symbolic conception of the political, argues that there is some kind of essence in man's nature.

> For there is such a thing as the Self, the Person—it does not yet exist but it must be attained, fought for against all those who are preventing its emergence and who substitute for it an illusory self, namely, the subject of voluntary servitude in production and consumption, the subject of free enterprise and free election of masters.[41]

But, for Marcuse, is there anything which is not historical in man's nature—in effect, is there such a conception of "man's nature" in Marcuse's thought? Is the entire attempt to place Marcuse in terms of this symbolic-therapeutic function of political philosophy fruitless? Doesn't the notion of a philosophic vision imply an essential something in human beings which is not historical, and is not this dimension lacking in Marcuse? When Marcuse argues that all is historical in man, he is arguing that man cannot be considered apart from the reality of his external situation. However, Marcuse believes that history itself can be changed. His belief in qualitative progress gives his vision a dimension which approximates an idea of sacred time, not as a separate reality, but in Eliade's original conception of a mode of being in the world, "Not regression to a previous stage of civilization, but return to an imaginary *temps perdu* in the real life of mankind."[42]

In a series of essays collected in *Five Lectures*, Marcuse contends that the Freudian formulation of the nature of man, like the link between necessity and freedom, is now "obsolete" because of changes in industrial society.[43] His vision is expressed in his distinction between quantitative and qualitative progress; and it is this distinction which can serve as an introduction to his discussion of time, the key to an understanding of his vision of a non-repressive reality.

Particularly characteristic of the modern view of progress is the evaluation of time. Time is understood as a straight line or endlessly rising curve, as a becoming that devalues all mere existence. The present is experienced with regard to the more or less uncertain future. The latter menaces the present from the beginning and is conceived and experienced with anxiety. The past remains behind as what can be neither mastered nor repeated but in such a way that it continues to determine the present just because it is unmastered. In this linearly expressed time, fulfilled time, the duration of gratification, the permanence of individual happiness, and time as peace can be represented only as superhuman or subhuman; as eternal bliss, which is possible and conceivable only after existence here on earth has ceased, or as the idea that the wish for the perpetuation of the happy moment is itself the inhuman or anti-human force that surrenders man to the devil.[44]

In Marcuse's vision, "time would not seem linear" but "cyclical, as the return contained in Nietzsche's idea of the 'perpetuity of pleasure.' "[45] In *Eros and Civilization*, Marcuse speaks approvingly of Nietzsche as one who "exposed the gigantic fallacy on which Western philosophy and morality were built."[46] Nietzsche exposed the fallacies that "culminated in the deification of time: because everything in the empirical world is passing, man is in his very essence a finite being, and death is the very essence of life."[47] Marcuse argues that "Nietzsche speaks in the name of a reality principle fundamentally antagonistic to that of Western civilization," that he breaks the "tyranny of becoming over being."[48] He sees time as the enemy of joyful being and realizes that the consignment of joy to a transcendental realm of being results in man's "slavery." Marcuse admires Nietzsche's symbol of the eternal return as a way of dealing with change which does not preclude life or make man an object of something higher or outside of man. Marcuse contends that, for Nietzsche, death *is*—it is conquered by willed re-creation and rebirth.

But why must Marcuse wage this battle against time? Marcuse argues that it is time that is the enemy of lasting gratification and human liberation. It is the flux of time which is society's ally in maintaining order. The individual learns from society to methodically resign himself, to deny himself a better future, and to accept conformity and the given institutional reality as what must be. The aesthetic state, in order to be the state of freedom, must defeat time's destructiveness; and it is Schiller's aesthetic dimension and play impulse which Marcuse deems appropriate for this task.

With alienated labor, man exists only part time, in his leisure time. Society's performance principle must constrict the unbounded pleasure principle. As Marcuse notes, society needs an organism "trained at its very roots."[49] The working day alienation and regimentation extend even into free time. Since the length of the work day is a prime societal regulatory agent, Marcuse argues that the reduction of the length of the working day is the first prerequisite for freedom.

Marcuse's symbol of Orpheus is of one who "defeats death." Marcuse must deal with death because it is this reality which "denies once and for all the reality of a non-repressive existence."[50] He links the attitude toward death to society's control but argues that death can become "a token of freedom."[51] For Marcuse, the Nirvana Principle and the reality principle do not have to be at odds if the instincts attain fulfillment in a non-repressive reality. The "biological rationale" of the "regression compulsion" would be lost.

But isn't Marcuse an historical thinker, and isn't time a necessary component of history? This assessment is correct in the sense that Marcuse believes that the nature of man is historically acquired. However, it is the second part of the question which is the most telling. Marcuse does not link time and history; and, in addition to attempting to eliminate the destructiveness of time as a category of man's existence, Marcuse radically argues that the nature of history itself is changeable. Marcuse would change history itself. To speak of the nature of man as historical is not to say, for Marcuse, that the nature of history cannot be changed.

Individuals reproduce repressive society in their needs, which persist even through revolution, and it is precisely this continuity which up to now has stood in the way of the leap from quantity into the quality of a free society. This idea implies that human needs have a historical character. All human needs, including sexuality, lie beyond the animal world. They are historically determined and historically mutable. And the break with the continuity of those needs that already carry repression with them, the leap into qualitative difference, is not a mere invention but inheres in the development of the productive forces themselves. That development has reached a level where it actually demands new vital needs in order to do justice to its own potentialities.[52]

Marcuse proposes a break in the historical continuum, the "letting of the realm of freedom appear within the realm of necessity."[53] Marcuse believes that it is now possible to speak of the end of utopia.

Utopia, as an historical concept, denotes social changes considered impossible because of the immaturity of the social situation. Certain subjective and objective factors of the situation prevent a transformation. Marcuse will now accept only one definition of utopia: that which implies a contradiction of real laws of nature, that is, eternal youth, return to a golden age. He argues that now all the material and intellectual forces are at hand for the realization of a free society. The abolition of poverty and misery are technically possible but are prevented by the total mobilization of society against its own liberation, a barrier consisting of the existing organization of the forces of production. An end of utopia would imply an end of history; that is, the new possibilities for a human society are no longer a continuation of the old or part of the same historical continuum. This is Marx's concept of a qualitative difference between an unfree and a free society, the former marking the "prehistory" of mankind. Marcuse would revise even Marx's idea of socialism as still tied to the idea of a continuum of progress and not the determinate negation of capitalism. The end of utopia necessitates a discussion of a new definition of socialism. A new qualitative difference could be attained wherein the realm of freedom could appear in the realm of necessity. He then proposes that "we must face the possibility that the path to socialism may proceed from science to utopia and not from utopia to science."[54]

For Marcuse, a new socialism connotes a new theory of man, a genesis and development of vital needs of and for freedom, for transformation, needs in a biological sense. This view implies the genesis of a new morality as the negation of the Judeo-Christian morality. It is the continuation of needs developed and satisfied in a repressive society that reproduces this society within the individuals. All human needs are historically determined and mutable (beyond basic physiological requirements). The productive forces are now developed enough to demand new, vital needs to realize their potential.

NOTES

1. Herbert Marcuse, *Reason and Revolution* (Boston: Beacon Press, 1941, paperback ed., 1960), p. 6.

2. Ibid., p. 9.

3. Ibid., p. 15.

4. Ibid., pp. 15-16.

5. Herbert Marcuse, "The Foundation of Historical Materialism (1932)," in *Studies in Critical Philosophy*, trans. Javis De Bres (Boston: Beacon Press, 1972), p. 21.

6. Ibid., p. 25.

7. Marcuse, *Reason and Revolution*, p. 267.

8. Ibid.

9. Herbert Marcuse, "Sartre's Existentialism (1948)," in *Studies in Critical Philosophy*, p. 183.

10. Herbert Marcuse, "Philosophy and Critical Theory (1937)," in *Negations* (Boston: Beacon Press, 1968), p. 137.

11. Ibid., p. 137.

12. Ibid., p. 139.

13. Ibid., p. 143.

14. Ibid., p. 154.

15. Ibid., p. 155.

16. Karl W. Deutsch, "On Political Theory and Political Action," *American Political Science Review* 65 (March 1971), p. 12.

17. Ibid.

18. Lee C. McDonald, "Myth, Politics, and Political Science," *Western Political Quarterly* 22 (March 1969), p. 145.

19. Ibid., p. 149.

20. Ibid., p. 147.

21. Michael Walzer, "On the Role of Symbolism in Political Thought," *Political Science Quarterly* 82 (June 1967), p. 194.

22. Elliot Zashin and Phillip C. Chapman, "The Uses of Metaphor and Analogy: Toward a Renewal of Political Language," *Journal of Politics* 36 (May 1974), p. 323.

23. Murray Edelman, *The Symbolic Uses of Politics* (Urbana: University of Illinois Press, 1964), p. 1.

24. Mircea Eliade, *Images and Symbols*, trans. Philip Mairet (New York: Sheed and Ward, 1961), p. 12.

25. Jolande Jacobi, *Complex/Archetype/Symbol*, trans. Ralph Manheim (New York: Pantheon Books, Inc., 1959), p. 88.

26. James M. Glass, "Plato, Marx, and Freud: Therapy, Eros, and the Rampage of Thanatos" (Paper delivered at the meeting of the Southern Political Science Association, Atlanta, Ga., November 1972), p. 1.

27. James M. Glass, "The Philosopher and the Shaman: The Political Vision as Incantation," *Political Theory* 2 (May 1974), p. 187.

28. Ibid., p. 189.

29. Ibid., p. 191.

30. Mircea Eliade, *The Sacred and the Profane*, trans. Willard R. Trask (New York: Harcourt, Brace and World, Inc., 1959), p. 69.

31. Ibid., p. 82.

32. Mircea Eliade, *Myths, Dreams, and Mysteries*, trans. Philip Mairet (New York: Harper and Row, 1957), p. 24.

33. R.D. Laing, *The Politics of Experience* (New York: Ballantine Books, 1967), p. 133.

34. Ibid., p. 137.

35. Ibid.

36. John G. Gunnell, *Political Philosophy and Time* (Middletown, Conn.: Wesleyan University Press, 1968), p. 249.

37. Ibid., p. 248.
38. Ibid., p. 252.
39. Ibid., p. 253.
40. Ibid., p. 11.
41. Herbert Marcuse, "Love Mystified: A Critique of Norman O. Brown (February 1967)," in *Negations*, p. 237.
42. Marcuse, *An Essay on Liberation*, p. 90.
43. Herbert Marcuse, "Obsolescence of the Freudian Concept of Man (1963)," in *Five Lectures* (Boston: Beacon Press, 1970), p. 46.
44. Herbert Marcuse, "Progress and Freud's Theory of Instincts (1968)," in *Five Lectures*, p. 32.
45. Ibid., p. 41.
46. Marcuse, *Eros and Civilization*, p. 109.
47. Ibid., p. 110.
48. Ibid.
49. Ibid., p. 43.
50. Ibid., p. 211.
51. Ibid., p. 216.
52. Herbert Marcuse, "The End of Utopia (1967)," in *Five Lectures*, p. 65.
53. Ibid., p. 63.
54. Ibid.

CHAPTER 4

The Therapeutic Vision
As Regeneration: Toward a
Marcuse-Jung Synthesis

Marcuse's therapeutic vision is one of regeneration. He conceives
of disease as a lack of tension, an absorption and diffusion of what
is phylogically and ontologically transcendent and oppositional.
A passage in *One-Dimensional Man* describes what Marcuse would
call a "sick" individual: "This identification is not illusion but
reality. However, the reality constitutes a more progressive stage
of alienation. The latter has become entirely swallowed up by its
alienated existence. There is only one dimension, and it is everywhere and in all forms."[1] He connects this view to the form of the
institutional reality:

The disharmony between the individual and the social needs, and the
lack of representative institutions in which the individuals work for themselves and speak for themselves, lead to the reality of such universals as
the Nation, the Party, the Constitution, the Corporation, the Church—
a reality which is not identical with any particular identifiable entity (individual, group, or institution). Such universals express various degrees
and modes of reification.[2]

This vision of a perverted Apollonian reality, a perverted vision
of the individual defined in the whole, can be found in *The Trial*
by Franz Kafka. Kafka expresses metaphorically the reality of one-
dimensional society. He presents, not in the language of philosophy
but in the language of prose, the reality of a non-comprehensible
reality devoid of negation and transcendence.

The world of Kafka's *Trial* is one in which the individual is unable to offer a critical alternative. In Marcuse's terms, Joseph K., as the *Trial* begins, is possessed of a "Happy Consciousness." He conceives of the world as ordered and reasonable: "Someone must have been telling lies about Joseph K., for without having done anything wrong he was arrested one fine morning."[3] The arrest was a mistake; an effect with a discoverable cause. Joseph K. could be confident that this was a temporary inconvenience and he could be secure in his belief that he lived in a country "with a legal constitution" where there was "universal peace" and where "all the laws were in force."[4] The wrong would be righted; and "once order was restored, every trace of these events would be obliterated and things would resume their old course."[5]

Joseph K.'s false consciousness led him to believe that he was an autonomous subject in his private sphere. Again it is possible to refer to Marcuse:

> The hypostatized whole resists analytic dissolution, not because it is a mythical entity behind the particular entities and performances but because it is the concrete, objective ground of their functioning in the given social and historical context. As such, it is a real force, felt and exercised by the individuals in their actions, circumstances, and relationships. They share in it (in a very unequal way); it decides on their existence and possibilities. The real ghost is of a very forcible reality—that of the separate and independent power of the whole over the individuals. And this whole is not merely a perceived *Gestalt* (as in psychology), nor a metaphysical absolute (as in Hegel), nor a totalitarian state (as in poor political science) —it is the established state of affairs which determines the life of the individuals.[6]

Joseph K. was a satisfied, contented producer, always prepared and confident at the bank. Gradually, his old sense of self-assurance in his private domain is sapped as the total administration infuses the public disorder into his private reality.[7] The mobilization of domination confronts the individual as impenetrable, "and the size of the Cathedral struck him as bordering on the limit of what human beings could bear."[8] He can neither reason nor feel; like Joseph K., another "resident" experienced this absorption. "The client ceased to be a client and became a lawyer's dog."[9]

Marcuse argues that conceptual thought alone is inadequate to "heal" Joseph K. and his diseased reality. If symbols have therapeutic power and relate to the totality of human experience, then it would appear that Joseph K. could draw on that function which would enable him to overcome his disease. However, Joseph K., like modern man, lacks access to symbols because of overemphasis on the conscious dimension. He is therefore unable to relate to his reality as a political actor in Gunnell's sense. That is, Joseph K. cannot use his capacity to function symbolically to create a rational political order out of the chaos of existence. Joseph K.'s existence lacks even the tension of chaos; it is a perverted, illusory political reality devoid of tension.

In *Philosophy in the Tragic Age of the Greeks*, Nietzsche argues that the Greeks invented the archetypes of philosophic thought.[10] Unlike Marcuse, Nietzsche did not believe that philosophy could serve a therapeutic purpose for a sick culture. For Nietzsche, philosophy could never be a reintegrative force in an already deteriorated culture.

In his *Birth of Tragedy*, Nietzsche identifies Apollo with illusion. Apollo the "god of all plastic energies is at the same time the soothsaying god."[11] He is the glorified ideal of unity and being; "Apollo, however, again appears to us as the apotheosis of the *principium individuationis*, in which alone is consummated the perpetually attained goal of the primal unity, its redemption through appearance."[12] With Apollo, the individual is determined in the general.

Apollo symbolizes self-control and knowledge of self. Apollo is a tranquilizing force; the individual exists in a dream of the redemptive power of knowledge and self. Pain is "veiled and withdrawn from sight."[13]

Nietzsche recognizes a second force at work in the world, for "behold: Apollo could not live without Dionysius."[14] Apollonian consciousness is recognized to be "like a veil" which "hid this Dionysian world from his vision."[15]

Dionysius excites the individual's symbolic faculties; his frenzied force tears down the veil of Apollo's illusion. With Dionysius, the individual again sinks into "oneness as the soul of the race and of nature itself." Man is no longer bounded, "He is no longer the artist, he has become a work of art."[16] Redemption is linked not with a knowledge of bounds and illusions or determination by the whole but with a natural and species reintegration.

A culture needs Apollo and Dionysius. Action requires illusion, and so Dionysius needs Apollo. Just as form requires content, Apollo needs Dionysius.

In his final work, Nietzsche identifies himself with Dionysius and Dionysius with the will to live.[17] Kaufmann argues that the Dionysius in *Ecce Homo* is different from the Dionysius of the *Birth of Tragedy*. He sees the Dionysius in *Ecce Homo* as passion controlled, as the synthesis of Dionysius and Apollo in *The Birth of Tragedy*.[18] Oddly enough, it is this "synthesis" Dionysius who speaks as a healer.

Marcuse's symbols of Orpheus and Narcissus are like the Nietzschean symbols in *The Birth of Tragedy*. Nietzsche was correct in *Philosophy in the Tragic Age of the Greeks*. Symbols such as these can do nothing for an ailing culture; they do not have the power. Marcuse's symbols, like Apollo and Dionysius, are doomed from the beginning. They are not bipolar, timeless, or limitless; rather, they are manifestations of the very reality principle they are to negate. What is puzzling in regard to Marcuse is his apparent recognition of the needed conceptualization of symbol. It would appear that there are sufficient grounds upon which to introduce a new definition of symbol into Marcuse's thought.

Marcuse speaks of a "subhistorical past when the life of the individual was the life of the genus," and his language occasionally hints at an acceptance of something beyond a personal unconscious.[19] This ambivalence is even more apparent when he notes that his image of Narcissus comes from the "mythological-artistic tradition rather than Freud's libido theory."[20] Marcuse's diagnosis almost seems to demand, logically, a definition of symbol which includes a reintegrative quality.

As a tentative definition of "sick society" we can say that a society is sick when its basic institutions and relations, its structure, are such they do not permit the use of the available material and intellectual resources for the optimal development and satisfaction of individual needs.[21]

In his preface to *Eros and Civilization*, Marcuse argues that instinctual liberation involves intellectual liberation; that is, the creation of an individual in a new, non-repressive reality involves the reintegration of modes of thought, feeling, and perception. Marcuse attempts to tap the healing power of symbols; he uses Orpheus and Narcissus as symbols of another reality principle. These images, as he sees them, reconcile Eros and Thanatos; and their aim is liberation, "the reunion of what has become separated."[22] Marcuse's symbols are inadequate to perform this function. If his attempts to provide a paradigm for a non-repressive reality through symbols validated in the aesthetic dimension are inadequate, then what alternate conception of symbol can be offered as a replacement?

Man's capacity as symbol maker has been widely discussed. Cassirer argues that a symbol is "a part of the human world of meaning."[23] Langer speaks of this need for symbols in people:

The heresy is this: that I believe there is a primary need in man, which all other creatures probably do not have, and which actuates all his apparently unzoological aims, his wistful fancies, his consciousness of value, his utterly impractical enthusiasms, and his awareness of a "Beyond" filled with holiness.[24]

Marcuse, in his attempt to stand in a therapeutic relationship to a diseased society, functions in what Jung would call the "visionary mode." Philipson argues that Jung hypothesizes that a certain type of art "functions for a society in a way analogous with the function of 'private' symbols in individual psychology."[25] This is what is known as the visionary mode of artistic creation. Works in the visionary mode function as symbols to compensate for a unidimensionality. Philipson believes that critical interpretation of art is for a culture what an analyst's interpretation of symbols is for a patient. With the right interpretation, a symbol can become a "living experience" possessed of potential reconciling and transcending power. A compensatory function is involved between the archetypes of the collective unconscious and consciousness. However, such details of the argument are premature at this stage. It is first necessary to explain the basis for this synthesis of Marcuse and Jung.[26] Marcuse himself rejects Jung outright as a pseudo-mythologist and reactionary.

For Jung, the unconscious has a positive, therapeutic value. Jung views the unconscious not as a "demonical monster" but as a "neutral," natural entity. Health is balance, and the therapeutic function relates to the reintegration of those elements which have been excluded. The danger coming from the unconscious is a function of the degree to which the unconscious has been ignored or repressed; the conscious mind is in more danger of being overwhelmed when the unconscious is ignored than when it attempts to relate to the unconscious.

For both Jung and Marcuse, therapy involves the reintegration of the unconscious as a curative for atrophied consciousness. Marcuse believes that scarcity is no longer a valid reason for repression, and Jung feels that the need to develop autonomy is no longer a valid reason for the repression of the unconscious. For Jung, the ego-conscious personality is not the whole person. Modern man is split off from the collective man and is even, at times, in opposition to him. Some degree of resistance to the unconscious is necessary for the development of both species and individual autonomy, but this quest for autonomy has become too one-sided. The situation is not without hope, however, for it is possible for the unconscious to compensate for over-intellectualized and rationalized modern consciousness:

> But since everything living strives for wholeness, the inevitable one-sidedness of our conscious life is continually being corrected and compensated by the universal human being in us, whose goal is the ultimate integration of conscious and unconscious, or better, the assimilation of the ego to a wider personality.[27]

This process of integration, or more properly in Jungian terminology "individuation," begins with conflict: "The self is made manifest in the opposites and in the conflict between them."[28] Basically, the psyche consists of personal and collective, conscious and unconscious elements. The collective unconscious is universal and objective. It "constitutes a common psychic substrate of a supra-personal nature which is present in every one of us."[29] The contents of the personal unconscious are the "feeling-toned complexes," while the contents of the collective unconscious are the "archetypes." Archetypes refer only to those contents which have not been consciously elaborated. The archetype is altered by becoming

conscious; its appearance is affected by the individual consciousness. Jung's instincts are "specifically formed motive forces." The
archetypes are "the unconscious images of the instincts themselves,
in other words, . . . they are *patterns of instinctual behavior*."[30]
Archetypes are inherited possibilities of ideas; the psyche, which for
Jung has the status of an autonomous reality, supplies the forms
that make possible the knowledge of objects.

Jung argues that "primitives," when faced with phenomena that
they could not understand, constructed myths and fairy tales to
serve as explanatory systems. Actually, Jung argues, these myths
and fairy tales were projections of psychic phenomena:

> He [primitive man] simply didn't know that the psyche contains all the
> images that have ever given rise to myths, and that our unconscious is an
> acting and suffering subject with an inner drama which primitive man
> rediscovers, by means of an analogy in the processes of nature both great
> and small.[31]

Jung contends that modern man uses dogma to replace the realities
of the processes of the collective unconscious. We use religious (and
in this case he speaks not of that impulse toward religion, but
dogma) rather than psychic explanations for events. This use, for
Jung, has resulted in an "impoverishment of symbols."

> I am convinced that the growing impoverishment of symbols has a
> meaning. It is a development that has an inner consistency. Everything
> that we have not thought about, and that has therefore been deprived
> of a meaningful connection with our developing consciousness, has got
> lost.[32]

Our symbols have lost meaning because we are ignorant of their
relation to our psychic processes. We receive symbols; we do not
realize that they come from within ourselves. Jung argues that we
accept this dogmatic condition because of a fear of "egocentric
subjectivity." In other words, if we "descend" into the unconscious
we will be overwhelmed by our own inadequacy and become
drowned in a sea of subjectivity without signposts or guides. But
for Jung, this is not a danger because the collective unconscious
is "sheer objectivity." Although we cannot know the collective

unconscious directly, we can be aware of its presence and its meaning for our existence. To those who would dismiss the importance
for human existence of considering unconscious elements because
of the futility of such a study (even after admitting the necessity
of such an enterprise), Jung would respond, "To ask the right
question is already half the solution of a problem."[33]

The argument for a Marcuse-Jung synthesis must establish Marcuse's belief in the importance of psychic factors. Such a synthesis
would be invalid if Marcuse could be shown to be concerned
exclusively with external-institutional reality; consciousness, then,
would be a reflection of institutional reality devoid of autonomy.

Marcuse doesn't regard consciousness as a mere reflection
of external forces. Indeed, he would argue that a change in consciousness must precede action. As he notes in *Counterrevolution
and Revolt*, "To prepare the ground for this development makes
the emancipation of consciousness still the primary task."[34]

The New Sensibility involves a change in the relationship between man and external nature. As described by Marcuse, the New
Sensibility is the medium for the integration of individual need
and social change. It is in the rediscovery of man's nature that the
drive for social change derives power. Nature is blocked as a
dealienating condition for man; in turn, nature is prevented from
being a subject in its own right. The liberation of nature, for Marcuse, is equivalent to the recovery of sensuous aesthetic qualities.

Marcuse argues that the early Marx was aware of this natural
basis for social change. Marcuse shows himself to be at odds with
most contemporary Marxists:

Marxist emphasis on the development of political consciousness shows
little concern with the roots of liberation in individuals, i.e., with the roots
of social relationships there where individuals most directly and pro-
foundly experience their world and themselves; in their *sensibility*, in their
instinctual needs.[35]

Marcuse concerns himself directly with consciousness, a concen-
tration he believes to be traceable to the young Marx. Marcuse
agrees that human nature would be different under socialism when
needs are developed and filled in an atmosphere of association, but

he disagrees with Marxists that "this change is to come about almost as a byproduct of the new socialist institutions."[36] He does not believe that the problem of a change in consciousness, that is, an individual change, can be avoided. Mutilated sense experience must be revitalized; sick individuals must be healed before they can begin to act. Marcuse focuses on the changes in consciousness as a prelude to institutional change. The sick individuals of our advanced industrial society have mutilated sense experience, and Marcuse's therapeutic goal is to recapture and reintegrate non-alienated modes of feeling and thinking. His therapeutic vision is epistemological:

"Radical sensibility": the concept stresses the active, constitutive role of the senses in shaping reason, that is to say, in shaping the categories under which the world is ordered, experienced, and changed. The senses are not merely passive, receptive: they have their own "syntheses" to which they subject the primary data of experience. And these syntheses are not only the pure "forms of intuition" (space and time) which recognized as an inexorable a priori *ordering* of sense data. There are perhaps also other syntheses, far more concrete, far more "material," which may constitute an empirical (i.e. historical) a priori of experience.[37]

Sensibility is blunted in a society based on alienated labor. The forms in which we perceive are given, and the existing society is reproduced in the senses and in the minds of the inhabitants. The old sensibility must be "dissolved," which is to say, there must be a second alienation of alienated man from the alienated society.

This view, however, presents Marcuse with a problem which he acknowledges. How can such an individual change be the basis for a universal change; or, in his words, "We are faced with the dialectic of the universal and the particular: how can the human sensibility, which is *principium individuationis,* also generate a *universalizing* principle?"[38] Marcuse's resolution of this dilemma solidifies the basis for a synthesis of his work with that of Jung. When Marcuse is confronted with a difficult question, he often turns to Hegel for strength. He would do well to turn to Jung, whom he has prematurely rejected. Often Marcuse seems to stretch Freud's theories beyond conceivable bounds to find the answers for which he is searching; but many of these answers can be found in Jung, without the "stretching." What follows is a discussion of Marcuse's resolution of the *principium individuationis* problem, demonstrating his debts to Hegel and Kant. It then will be shown that Jung's concepts of archetype and collective unconscious offer a solution to the problem with which Marcuse is concerned. Not only can Jung be helpful to Marcuse with this particular problem, but he can serve to augment and elaborate Marcuse's therapeutic vision.

Marcuse is concerned with the problem of universality when predicating liberation on what he refers to as the individual sensibility. His resolution of this problem is strongly influenced by his reading of Hegel. In *Reason and Revolution*, Marcuse asked of Hegel what he would ask of himself in *Counterrevolution and Revolt*: "Does the structure of individual reasoning (the subjectivity) yield any general laws and concepts that might constitute universal standards of rationality? Can a universal rational order be built upon the autonomy of the individual?"[39] The notions of universality and objectivity are vital to Marcuse's therapeutic vision. If man is to have the potential to transcend his given concrete existence, he must be capable of standing in opposition to this reality. He must, in other words, have the ability to function in a manner which can formulate standards against which he can compare his condition. Thinking would appear not to meet the criteria of universality since it varies with individuals, but for Hegel there is a totality of objective concepts and principles which he calls reason. It is reason which can provide a "guiding principle for the common organization of life."[40] For Hegel, the ego is integrative; it takes all the existential conditions and absorbs them into its own self-identity. The problem of universality is resolved in the functioning of the individual ego. Marcuse argues that this is the process which modern society blocks; the individual is not permitted to autonomously reproduce his society. A mimetic process replaces the constitutive, ordering process. There is no conscious collective action. While in a "healthy" society, the individual would dialectically interact with his reality, in the one-dimensional society the individual's identification is complete and immediate because the scope of this society's power and influence is complete and immediate.

In modern society, Marcuse argues, freedom is negative, for it finds its refuge not in the collectivity but in the individual ego. Marcuse, like Hegel, contends that in order to attain positive freedom the individual must transcend private interest and locate himself in the universality of his will.

The emancipation of the senses is the beginning and foundation for universal liberation. Kant, Marcuse argues, attempted to provide—through his notion of universal categories—the basis for an objective, universal freedom in the individual. Hegel introduces society and history into the equation. For Hegel, sense-certainty becomes perception; and in perception the "subject constitutes the objectivity of the thing."[41] Hegel discovered a "We" in the "I" of intuition and perception. For Hegel, full human existence comes in social life; individual liberation becomes predicated upon the liberation of society. For Marcuse, Hegel, through the introduction of history and society into the discussion of freedom, set aside an abstract approach which focused on the individual apart from the social condition. Marcuse admires the materialist elements in Feuerbach's and Kierkegaard's existentialism for embodying traits of a social theory, but he asserts that it is only with Marx that there is a radical break with earlier philosophic and religious speculations on the connection between universality and the individual.

According to Marcuse, Marx alone reconciled human freedom and natural necessity, subjective and objective freedom. The liberation of nature involves the recognition of fundamental "truths" in nature. The Marxian vision, as interpreted by Marcuse, "recaptures the ancient theory of knowledge as *recollection*."[42] This rediscovery of forms recognizes symbols which can indicate new, nonperverted syntheses. The emancipation of the senses would result in the universality of freedom as an objective human need, a universal objective need for freedom.

Freedom, says Marcuse, will come to be defined as the drive to enhance the life instincts.[43] The emancipation of the senses, he concludes, is the beginning of and foundation for universal liberation.

Marcuse argues that this recollected material, envisioned by Marx, has been consigned to imagination and sanctioned in higher culture in modern society. However, when these images are released, they can provide the needed new syntheses: "These images

may well be called 'innate ideas' inasmuch as they cannot possibly
be given in the immediate experience which prevails in the repressive societies."[44] Marcuse is concerned with the therapeutic function of political philosophy; he views political philosophy as standing in a critical and transcendent relationship to the existing reality.
He argues that the creation of an individual in a new, non-repressive reality involves the reintegration of modes of thought, feeling,
and perception. Sickness is one-dimensionality, a perverted Apollonian reality, a perverted vision of the individual defined in the
whole. Marcuse's therapeutic vision would release qualities heretofore confined to the realm of "higher culture" for incorporation
into material existence. He sees the emergence of a new reality
principle under which a new aesthetic ethos would be created. It is
in an objective aesthetic dimension that Marcuse finds a model for
his vision: "And it is precisely here that, if we are looking for a concept that can perhaps indicate the qualitative difference in socialist
society, the aesthetic-erotic [sic] dimension comes to mind almost
spontaneously, at least to me"[45]

The aesthetic values can come into play because of the dialectic.
This reintegrative power that was spoken about in *Eros and
Civilization* was set up to be freed by the apparently repressive
desublimation of *One-Dimensional Man*. Marcuse saw in *One-
Dimensional Man* the liquidation of two-dimensional culture. The
cultural values produced on a mass scale were becoming the agents
of social cohesion. Those elements which stood in opposition to
the established reality, including the cultural elements, were being
absorbed by the one-dimensional society. Marcuse traces the roots
of this development to the evolution of idealist thought.

As Marcuse understands it (and here he speaks specifically of
Aristotle), ancient philosophy linked knowledge to practice. Only
philosophy as a form of knowledge existed for its own sake. The
useful was separated from the beautiful, and the necessary was
consigned to a dimension of uncertainty and change. Happiness
could be found only in a dimension where philosophy exists. The
material world became devalued because it was the realm of
change, chaos, and flux. The soul was divided into higher and
lower parts, sensuality and reason. For Marcuse, this division
resulted from the same motivation as the prior separation of the

useful and the beautiful, the fear of change. Sensuality, like the material world, became devalued through this separation.

Marcuse follows these divisions through the development of Western thought. He contends that the material world, in this idealist tradition, becomes unreal or real only as far as it participates in, is influenced by, or is formed by the Idea(s). Marcuse criticizes Hegel for confusing a specific historical arrangement of the material world with what the latter believed to be the embodiment of an eternal form.

In his indictment of Western consciousness, Marcuse ties his conception of the separation of the useful and the beautiful and sense and reason to the dominant mode of the bourgeois culture. "Culture" develops as a concept representing the spiritual world as opposed to the material world of "civilization." Culture is removed from the social process. There is a reversal among the bourgeois of the ancient attitude toward the beautiful. For Marcuse, this reversal is insidious because it is linked to repression and co-optation. Culture, as seen by the bourgeois, is not the domain of a particular stratum or profession but it is "universal"; and all the individuals should experience and participate in cultural values. Culture can pacify the troubles of civilization, a condition Marcuse calls "affirmative culture":

By affirmative culture is meant that culture of the bourgeois epoch which led in the course of its own development to the segregation from civilization of the mental and spiritual world as an independent realm of value that is also considered superior to civilization.[46]

Anxiety about happiness was responsible for the original separations. For Marcuse, this original separation of the useful and the beautiful set the stage for the subsequent devaluation of the material mode of existence. For the ancients, he argues, "What man is to find in the philosophical knowledge of the true, the good, and the beautiful is ultimate pleasure, which has all the opposite characteristics of material facticity: permanence in change, purity amidst impurity, freedom amidst unfreedom."[47]

Abstract equality of bourgeois man promises a new happiness

for all, which for Marcuse is an illusion denying the built-in ine-
qualities of the bourgeois system of production. Affirmative culture came to conceal real suffering. Humanity becomes linked to
ideas in culture in which all can participate. This "inner state" does
not conflict with material existence. The soul, which does not have
exchange value, can't be hurt by what goes on in the material
world: "The freedom of the soul was used to excuse the poverty,
martyrdom, and bondage of the body."[48] Affirmative culture subjects sensuality to the domination of the soul. The soul is set off
and against the body. The soul is special; it cannot be sullied by the
chaos of the real world: "By being incorporated into spiritual life,
sensuality is to be harnessed and transfigured."[49]

Marcuse's description of the development of "affirmative culture" culminates in the picture of a modern industrial bourgeois
society in which we have a perverted system of perception. We can,
however, recapture or recollect, through our imagination, new
syntheses for our sense experiences.

Other similarities between Marcuse and Jung now become apparent. Marcuse's "innate ideas" can be said to correspond to Jung's
"archetypes" in proposed structure and function. This is a point
that will be returned to shortly. However, Marcuse's innate ideas,
like Jung's archetypes, are without substance themselves; they
serve only to provide form for the synthesis of the sense experience. Marcuse again approximates Jung with his contention that
these images (innate ideas) cannot "possibly be given in the immediate experience which prevails in the repressive societies."[50]
Jungian archetypes are not the product of repressed individual or
personal experience, but are universal collectivities which have an
objective existence. For Marcuse, the innate ideas are the *"horizon*
of experience under which the immediate given norms of things
appear as 'negative,' as denial of their inherent possibilities, their
truth."[51] Jungian archetypes are inherited through patterns which
are devoid of specific content but when tapped give form to perception and thought.[52] Marcuse's innate ideas are historical; but, in
a sense, so are Jung's archetypes, which are "the deposits of the
constantly repeated experiences of humanity."[53]

The unconscious has a positive therapeutic function for Jung.
Marcuse's innate ideas give his vision the ability to conceive of

individual liberation in terms of objective universals. These innate ideas can serve as the needed syntheses, the needed basis for the new sensibility. For Marcuse, these syntheses do exist, but they are in the realm of higher culture. Marcuse returns to Marx, who spoke of forming the object world "in accordance with the laws of beauty."[54] Marcuse conceives of aesthetic qualities as being "nonviolent and nondomineering." He argues that recaptured, aesthetic needs can counter aggressiveness and result in freedom because a precondition of freedom for Marcuse is receptivity.

Marcuse is concerned with the transformative potentialities of art. The aesthetic form represents a needed new harmonious synthesis. Art transcends, without eliminating, class conflict. Marcuse doesn't call for the end of art but for the end of the affirmative character of culture through which art justifies and supports the existing order. The affirmative character of art was too easily absorbed and co-opted by the existing reality. Art, however, maintains an alienated, idealized relation to reality. Even the world of illusion, because it is such, retains a subversive reality. Art is recollection; it speaks to undistorted modes of experience and perception as opposed to "instrumentalist reason and sensibility."[55] Art is in danger of losing its transcendence when it becomes a part of real life. How can art become a guide to change; that is, how can the cultural revolution become an element of praxis without losing its transcendent force? To put the dilemma in other terms: can symbols validated in the aesthetic dimension maintain a critical tension when they are activated in concrete conscious existence? The tension has to remain between art and reality; art can never become reality. Marcuse's resolution of this problem becomes clearer when conceived of and rephrased in Jungian terms.

What is intolerable for Marcuse is the unity of opposites, the elimination of dialectical tension. For Jung, too, progress in life can come only through the tension of opposites.[56] Odajnyk, who explores the political implications of Jung's work, states that the individual in Jung's system is in the center of an energy system: "He is the center around which revolve the various oppositions and tensions—spirit and matter, instinct and inheritance, individual and group—that are conducive to the production of psychic energy."[57]

This Jungian tension can charge Marcuse's symbols. Marcuse, by positing only a personal unconscious, restricts his symbols to contents which have passed through the repressive society. The symbols themselves then become reflections of individual repressive experiences. Jung's collective unconscious, like Marcuse's aesthetic dimension, has universality and objectivity. Marcuse himself prepares the way for his synthesis with Jung by positing the existence of innate ideas which can revitalize distorted individual perception. Jung's archetypes, which are the contents of the collective unconscious, are the psychological equivalent of Marcuse's innate ideas. Jung's symbols, as external manifestations of the archetypes, can revitalize Marcuse's vision.

Odajnyk notes that it is the symbol in Jung's system which transforms surplus psychic energy into cultural manifestations. Symbol formation itself is an unconscious process, but symbols are available to consciousness. Symbols provide "the psychic and the organizational foundations of social life."[58] Jung regards symbols as energy transformers; they can convert libido from a lower to a higher form. A symbol receives its power from the tension generated as it strives against instinctual resistance.[59]

Symbols, in the Jungian sense, facilitate the healing function of the therapeutic vision. They can reconcile pairs of opposites: conscious and unconscious, form and content, masculine and feminine. A symbol is, in a sense, a mediator between the conscious and unconscious. It has a healing function as a "transformer of energy."[60] A symbol can halt the regression of the libido into the unconscious. The actual process of gaining access to symbols can be a reintegrating one.

Jung argues that a doctor must deal with the unconscious and the conscious aspects of a patient's personality. It is imperative that the political philosopher recognize the power of unconscious realities. Political philosophy cannot continue to conceive of man as "simplex" rather than "duplex."[61] For Jung, self-knowledge is not identical with ego-consciousness. He contends that we can only guard against psychic infection if we know what is attacking us. Theories based on statistics falsify reality by glossing over individual differences.

Rational philosophy, for Jung, does not allow for the existence of what Jung calls the "shadow." Jungian man is composed naturally of good and evil; and to attempt to deny the presence of this evil is to deny an aspect of existence, a process which can be particularly dangerous since modern technology facilitates the realization of this evil to a heretofore unparalleled degree.

It is imperative that human knowledge continually evolve to meet the changing demands of a changing reality. We must not stop the flow of instinctual energy into our existence, as is happening in one-dimensional society. This tension of opposites and the accompanying energy has been stifled. Philosophy can become powerful if it taps the archetypal energy; then, the therapeutic vision of the political philosopher will take into account conscious and unconscious dimensions of existence. Marcuse's vision, then, can meet the challenge seen by Jung: "If the flow of instinctive dynamism into our life is to be maintained, as is absolutely necessary for our existence, then it is imperative we remould these archetypal forms into ideas which are adequate to the challenge of the present."[62]

This chapter has advanced several important arguments, and it is worthwhile to recapitulate and elaborate some of its major points.

Again we can ask: why does Marcuse reject Jung? Initially, Marcuse attacks Jung's lack of awareness of the effects of a repressive external reality. Marcuse denounces Jung as a right wing psychoanalyst who holds the belief that a person can be healthy and creative even in a repressive reality. But this seems to be a minor criticism. Since Marcuse's work of late has evolved more in the direction of changes in consciousness than direct political actions, this seems to be less than a devastating attack. If Marcuse can believe that the Great Refusal can occur within the old society and that the New Sensibility can be formed as a precondition for revolution, then Jung can believe that individuation can precede direct external institutional change.

But again, this is not Marcuse's most fundamental criticism of Jung. Marcuse argues that Jung reduces the role of the instinctual dynamic in the life of the psyche. "Thus purified, the psyche can again be redeemed by idealistic ethics and religion; and the psychoanalytic theory of the mental apparatus can be written as a philosophy of the soul."[63] Glover, to whom Marcuse refers, can be helpful here. Marcuse dismisses Jung after a few comments by referring the reader to Glover's *Freud or Jung?*, a piece highly critical of Jung. Glover argues that Jung's psychology, which employs a conception of libido as psychic energy, is one-dimensional; that is, it "flattens out" the more specific meanings found in Freud. Glover is primarily concerned with what he believes to be Jung's failure to adequately explain certain processes: namely, why some of the contents of the collective unconscious are expressed in consciousness while others are not, how the contents of the personal unconscious become repressed, and how consciousness is influenced by these processes. These questions introduce certain matters of a technical nature which cannot be dealt with here. What is important in Glover's argument in terms of this study is his criticism of Jung's conception of symbol. Glover accurately states the difference between Jung and Freud in this regard:

> Phantasy, he [Jung] maintained, is causally explained as a symptom of a physiological or personal condition. A symbol purposively seeks a clear and definite goal with the help of existing material; it strives to lay hold of a certain line for the future psychic development.[64]

For Freud, Glover argues, a symbol is a concrete representation of a more inaccessible idea, not of an abstract idea.

Ernest Jones, a Freudian, concurs with Glover. He contends that Jung makes the concept of symbol meaningless. In other words, a symbol, as he reads Jung, comes to mean "any mental process that is substituted for another."[65] Jones argues that Jung's work on the anagogic signification of symbols becomes lost in a maze of mysticism and occultism. Jung, states Jones, abandons science, particularly the principles of causality and determinism. Jones believes that the similarity Jung finds in symbols is due not to inheritance but to the uniformity of the human mind.

These charges of mysticism and occultism refer to what Marcuse calls Jung's abuse of the truth value of imagination. Marcuse argues that Jung emphasizes the retrospective qualities of imagination. Jung, for Marcuse, has eliminated the critical insights of Freud's theory.

Although Marcuse favors Freud's conceptions of fantasy and

symbol, he must revise them. It is interesting that while Marcuse appears to cling to Freud, he actually—although he would strongly deny this—moves closer to Jung. Marcuse's own conceptions of fantasy and symbol are at best distortions of Freud's original intentions.

Freud, Marcuse argues, restores imagination to its rights: "As a fundamental, independent mental process, fantasy has a truth value of its own, which corresponds to an experience of its own— namely, the surmounting of the antagonistic reality."[66] Marcuse realizes that Freud's recognition of fantasy as a thought process wasn't original, but he argues that Freud did attempt to show the "genesis of this mode of thought and its essential connection with the pleasure principle."[67] For Freud, the mental forces that oppose the reality principle reside mainly in the unconscious. Fantasy, for Freud, unlike the pleasure principle, operates in the "developed consciousness" and still maintains autonomy in relation to the reality principle. Furthermore, fantasy "preserves the archetypes of the genus, the perpetual but repressed ideas of the collective and individual memory, the tabooed images of freedom."[68] Fantasy retains the structures of the original, undifferentiated psyche and preserves the memory of the subhistorical past, "the image of the immediate unity between the universal and the particular under the rule of the pleasure principle."[69] The ego is guided only by consciousness: "as *reason* it becomes the sole repository of judgment, truth, rationality; it decides what is useful and useless, good and evil."[70] But this is a distorted ego; the establishment of the reality principle mutilates the mind. The mental processes were unified in the pleasure ego and are not split:

Thus conditioned, this part of the mind obtains the monopoly of interpreting, manipulating, and altering reality—of governing remembrance and oblivion, even of defining what reality is and how it should be used and altered. The other part of the mental apparatus remains free from the control of the reality principle—at the price of becoming powerless, inconsequential, unrealistic.[71]

Why does Marcuse need to revise Freud? Quite simply, he realizes that the function he desires for fantasy (described in the preceding section) is not directly found in Freud. Freud does not believe in the possibility of a non-repressive reality principle. Ironically, Marcuse admires Freud, who thinks a non-repressive reality is a form of retrogression, but attacks Jung for this very reason. How does Marcuse resolve this apparent dilemma? He believes there are grounds in Freud's own theory to revise the latter's belief in the inevitability of the link between civilization and repression.

Marcuse bases his revision on Freud's notion of narcissism:

> If this is the case, then all sublimation would begin with the reactivation of narcissistic libido, which somehow overflows and extends to objects. The hypothesis all but revolutionizes the idea of sublimation: it hints at a non-repressive mode of sublimation which results from an extension rather than a constraining deflection of the libido.[72]

Marcuse argues that narcissism, usually connected with egoistic withdrawal from reality, is actually connected with oneness, "a fundamental relatedness to reality which may generate a comprehensive existential order."[73] It is narcissism which could contain the "germ" for a new reality principle: "The libidinal cathexis of the ego (one's own body) may become the source and reservoir for a new libidinal cathexis of the objective world—transforming this world into a new mode of being."[74] Marcuse's images of Orpheus and Narcissus are images of the Great Refusal, a refusal to "accept separation from the libidinous object (or subject)."[75] Marcuse would rescue fantasy and reconnect it with Eros. He argues that Freud's dichotomy between the sexual instincts and fantasy was surpassed in the later reformulation of the instinct theory. Marcuse reasons that after culture has done its work, has provided a model for a non-repressive reality, mankind could be free. This regression, he argues, differs from that of Jung, for it would be "in the light of a mature consciousness and guided by a new rationality."[76]

Certain questions must be asked of Marcuse: what does he "expect" from fantasy; what wasn't in Freud that he had to add; could he have found this in Jung without the corrections he had to make to Freud; and isn't he distorting Freud beyond all reasonable bounds?

The last question appears to be answered by Marcuse himself.

He realizes that he must revise Freud because of the following difficulty:

> However, according to Freud, the image conjures only the *subhistorical* past of the genus (and of the individual) prior to all civilization. Because the latter can develop only through the destruction of the subhistorical unity between pleasure principle and reality principle, the image must remain buried in the unconscious, and imagination must become mere phantasy, child's play, daydreaming. The long road of consciousness which led from the primal horde to ever higher forms of civilization cannot be reversed.[77]

When Marcuse argues that fantasy is a thought process, he means that it has "its own laws and truth values."[78] Marcuse sees the unity that can be redeemed by fantasy as real, not illusion but knowledge. For Marcuse, fantasy creates a universe (in art) that is subjective and objective. Formerly, the potentials of a non-repressive reality had been consigned to art, in political philosophy —utopian speculation. But the domination, he would argue, has never been complete; fantasy has remained a truth incompatible with reason.

> The categories in which philosophy has comprehended the human existence have retained the connection between reason and suppression: whatever belongs to the sphere of sensuousness, pleasure, impulse has the connotation of being antagonistic to reason—something that has to be subjugated, constrained.[79]

Marcuse argues that Jung's conception of fantasy is purely retrogressive, that is, it reaches only to the subhistorical past and lacks any future orientation. Why is this point important to Marcuse? It appears that Marcuse wants not a return to a primordial time but a time after the new rationality and sensibility have prepared the way for a different and non-repressive reality principle for modern industrial society. He argues that Jung's conception of fantasy is limited to a regression to a primitive state of mind and being. Marcuse misreads Jung.

Jung argues that Freud "reduces" the concepts of symbol and fantasy and offers a purely causal explanation of their nature and function. For Jung, every psychological fact is always becoming and creative: "The psychological moment is Janus-faced—it looks both backwards and forwards. Because it is becoming, it also prepares for the future event."[80] Fantasy, he states, has to be understood purposively as well as causally. To speak solely in causal terms is to speak not of symbols but of symptoms—symbols have a future orientation, symptoms do not. According to Jung, Freud's "symbols" are actually symptoms or signs and lack any future orientation. More directly, Jung recognizes that symbols must have a future direction; Freud denies this role directly, a role Marcuse deems vital for the therapeutic function of symbols. Fantasy, for Jung, combines feeling, thought, intuition, and sensation, in other words, all the functions of the psyche. Jung believes that both Adler and Freud reject imagination because they reduce fantasies to semiotic expressions. For Jung, what Freud calls symbols are actually signs for elementary instinctive processes. Marcuse seems to be unable to accept the logical conclusion that it is Jung, rather than Freud, who has the more powerful, transcendent conceptions of symbol and fantasy.

In addition, Jung's conceptions of art and creativity show more of a relationship to Marcuse's than to Freud's. For Marcuse, the aesthetic dimension is the repository of certain truths, the domain of certain non-perverted forms which can serve as the model for the needed syntheses to heal the mutilated sense experience and lead to the new rationality and sensibility. Creative inspiration for Freud involves the artist's ability to tap the lost images and feelings of his or her childhood. For Freud, the artist has powerful instinctual demands which he or she cannot satisfy. These must be expressed in a fantasy world "on the borderline of neurosis."[81] Marcuse had to revise Freud. Freud locates much of this creative function in consciousness and in the ego, and this is the domain which Marcuse sees as the most repressed and the most distorted. Marcuse admires Freud's connection of the aesthetic dimension with the pleasure principle. However, he cannot (without substantially distorting Freud) argue that Freud's conception of aesthetics is grounded in a realm free from the dominant reality principle. Spector, who is concerned with a discussion of Freudian aesthetics, emphasizes this factor:

When we try to locate art within this scheme, we conclude that the seat of aesthetic activity must be in the ego, judging from Freud's remark that although the ego draws its energies from the id, what distinguishes the ego from the id is "a disposition for synthesizing its contents, for concentrating and unifying the emotions, completely missing in the id."[82]

For Jung, the unconscious has a creative, therapeutic value. Culture represents not a substitution for instinctual pleasure but an autonomous force.

According to Kaplan, Freud brings within the domain of nature and science "much of what traditional aesthetics assigned to a transcendent metaphysics."[83] Now Marcuse might argue that Jung falls into mysticism, but he cannot deny that he himself holds what Kaplan refers to as a "traditional aesthetic" theory. Recall Marcuse's comments on the separation of the useful and the beautiful and the resulting consignment, on the part of the boureois, of the aesthetic truths to a "higher" and therefore harmless domain. Freud is one of the bourgeoisie whom Marcuse criticizes. Freud separates the useful and the beautiful and does not believe, like Marcuse and Jung, that aesthetic values are "real." As Freud notes:

This aesthetic attitude to the goal of life offers little protection against the threat of suffering, but it can compensate for a great deal. The enjoyment of beauty has a peculiar, mildly intoxicating quality of feeling. Beauty has no obvious use; nor is there any clear cultural necessity for it. Yet civilization could not do without it [as a means of substitute gratification].[84]

Marcuse criticizes Aristotle's and Kant's deprecation of fantasy; he should—but does not—include Freud in his indictment.[85] Freud supposedly removes aesthetics from this separate realm with his formulation of an unconscious.[86] Marcuse is a materialist and is therefore attracted to this stance. However, it is Jung rather than Freud who provides a synthesis between idealist aesthetics and material existence.

Jung's symbols have a unifying function. For Jung, fantasy is "the creative soil for everything that has ever brought development to humanity."[87] Jung has a hermeneutic conception of symbols:

For the significance of a symbol is not that it is a disguised indication of something that is generally known, but that it is an endeavor to elucidate by analogy what is as yet completely unknown and only in process of formation. The phantasy represents to us that which is just developing under the form of a more or less apposite analogy. By analytical reduction to something universally known, we destroy the actual value of the symbol; but it is appropriate to its value and meaning to give it an hermeneutical interpretation.[88]

Jung's psychological mode of artistic creation (and this seems to be close to Freud's conception of artistic creation) deals with material from the realm of human consciousness. In contrast, the experience that furnishes the material for the visionary mode is not familiar. The visionary mode, in the sense that it taps a non-perverted dimension, parallels Marcuse's conception of the nature of creation in the aesthetic dimension. Marcuse is aware that Jung recognizes the radical implications of such a process: "The idealistic and aesthetic sublimations which prevail in Schiller's work do not vitiate its radical implications. Jung recognized these implications and was duly frightened by them."[89] Marcuse argues that the New Sensibility will involve a radical break in consciousness. Jung indeed is aware of the potential strength of this force. In his own words, he warns:

These never rend the curtain that veils the cosmos: they never transcend the bounds of the humanly possible, and for this reason are readily shaped to the demands of art, no matter how great a shock to the individual they may be. But the primordial experiences rend from top to bottom the curtain upon which is painted the picture of an ordered world, and allow a glimpse into the unfathomed abyss of what has not yet become.[90]

Jung does not see creation in the visionary mode as derived or secondary; it is "a true symbolic expression—that is, the expression of something existent in its own right, but imperfectly known."[91] What appears in this vision is the collective unconscious. Man as an artist is man in a collective sense. Although there is a danger that functioning in this mode contradicts free will, this mode is genuinely therapeutic in Marcuse's sense.

The secret of artistic creation and the effectiveness of art is to be found in a return to the state of *participation mystique*—to that level of experience at which it is man who lives, and not the individual, and at which the weal or woe of the single human being does not count, but only human existence.[92]

Ira Progoff explores the social meaning of Jung's psychology. One of his conclusions is that when social symbols no longer function effectively, the individual turns or is turned back into himself. When the dominant consciousness breaks up or is weakened, material which has heretofore been unassimilated is brought to the surface. Without satisfying symbols, a society cannot hold together. As Progoff notes:

Without taking the point further than a psychological formulation, Jung maintains the basic thesis that a society can continue to function effectively only by providing its individuals with meanings in which they can have a living faith. Only then can the psychic energies be directed out into the world and in to the socially productive enterprises which a community requires. If a culture fails to maintain psychologically effective symbols, its individuals withdraw from the social areas of life and turn into themselves in search of new meanings.[93]

A political philosopher can tap the healing power of symbols but cannot create. Neither the individual nor the society can make a dead symbol live again. A symbol must come to the individual from the psyche; "It cannot be deliberately and consciously developed, not can it be intellectually worked out and rationally believed in."[94] Where there is disintegration, the symbol can create a new center; but it appears that the political philosopher cannot in this sense "create" the symbol.[95]

Does this mean that it is impossible to speak of the therapeutic function of political philosophy? Not at all. But what about the problem of symbol formation? If symbols can only arise spontaneously, isn't the political philosopher unable to create symbols which can "heal" the diseased reality? Jung argues that the person who is in touch with his unconscious cannot help but affect his circumstances and those around him. Marcuse, too, argues that utopian speculation is merely the elaboration of concrete historical possibilities. This explains the function of the political philosopher. The therapeutic function of political philosophy speaks to all dimensions of human existence. When the political philosopher is able to tap the unconscious, which for Marcuse would be the aesthetic dimension, he can elaborate symbols which can have a therapeutic effect upon the society.

NOTES

1. Marcuse, *One-Dimensional Man*, p. 11.

2. Ibid., p. 206.

3. Franz Kafka, *The Trial*, trans. Willa Muir and Edwin Muir (New York: Schocken Books, 1968), p. 1.

4. Ibid., p. 5.

5. Ibid., p. 17.

6. Marcuse, *One-Dimensional Man*, p. 207.

7. Marcuse, *Eros and Civilization*, p. XVII.

8. Kafka, *The Trial*, pp. 208-209.

9. Ibid., p. 193.

10. Friedrich Nietzsche, *Philosophy in the Tragic Age of the Greeks*, trans. Marianne Cowan (Chicago: Henry Regnery Company, A Gateway Edition, 1962), p. 31.

11. Friedrich Nietzsche, *The Birth of Tragedy* (1872), trans. Walter Kaufmann (New York: Vintage Books, 1967), p. 35.

12. Ibid., p. 45.

13. Ibid., p. 42.

14. Ibid., p. 46.

15. Ibid., p. 41.

16. Ibid., pp. 37.

17. Friedrich Nietzsche, *Ecce Homo* (1908), ed. Oscar Levy, trans. Anthony M. Ludovici (New York: Russell and Russell, Inc., 1964), p. 72.

18. Walter Kaufmann, *Nietzsche* (New York: Vintage Books, 1968), p. 129.

19. Marcuse, *Eros and Civilization*, pp. 129, 191.

20. Ibid., p. 152.

21. Herbert Marcuse, "Aggressiveness in Advanced Industrial Society" (date not given), in *Negations*, p. 251.

22. Marcuse, *Eros and Civilization*, pp. 149, 154.

23. Ernst Cassirer, *An Essay on Man* (New Haven: Yale University Press, 1944), p. 32.

24. Susanne K. Langer, *Philosophy in a New Key* (1942) (Cambridge, Mass.: Harvard University Press, 1963), p. 40.

25. Morris Philipson, *An Outline of a Jungian Aesthetics* (Evanston: Northwestern University Press, 1963), p. 102.

26. The possibility of such a synthesis has been discussed by Weber in Shierry M. Weber, "Individuation as Praxis," in *Critical Interruptions: New Left Perspectives on Herbert Marcuse*, ed. Paul Breines (New York: Herder and Herder, Inc., 1970), pp. 37-38.

27. Carl G. Jung, *Dreams*, trans. R.F.C. Hull, Bollingen Series 20, Vols. 4, 8, 12, 16 (Princeton: Princeton University Press, 1974), p. 78.

28. Ibid., p. 260.

29. C.G. Jung, *The Archetypes and the Collective Unconscious*, trans. R.F.C. Hull, Bollingen Series 20, Vol 9 (Princeton: Princeton University Press, 1974), p. 4.

30. Ibid., p. 44.

31. Ibid., p. 7.

32. Ibid., p. 14.

33. Ibid., p. 23.

34. Herbert Marcuse, *Counterrevolution and Revolt* (Boston: Beacon Press, 1972), p. 132.

35. Ibid., p. 62.

36. Ibid.

37. Ibid., p. 63.

38. Ibid., p. 72.

39. Marcuse, *Reason and Revolution*, p. 18.

40. Ibid., p. 7.

41. Ibid., p. 107.

42. Marcuse, *Counterrevolution and Revolt*, p. 69.

43. Ibid., p. 71.

44. Ibid., p. 70.

45. Marcuse, "The End of Utopia," in *Five Lectures*, p. 68.

46. Herbert Marcuse, "Affirmative Character of Culture (1937)," in *Negations*, p. 95.

47. Ibid., p. 96.

48. Ibid., p. 109.

49. Ibid., p. 110.

50. Marcuse, *Counterrevolution and Revolt*, p. 70.

51. Ibid.

52. C.G. Jung, *Two Essays on Analytical Psychology*, trans. R.F.C. Hull, Bollingen Series 20, Vol 7 (Princeton: Princeton University Press, 1953), p. 138.

53. Marcuse, *Counterrevolution and Revolt*, p. 70; Jung, *Two Essays*, p. 69.

54. Marcuse, *Counterrevolution and Revolt*, p. 74.

55. Ibid., p. 99.

56. Jung, *Two Essays*, p. 53.

57. Walter Odajnyk, "The Political Ideas of C.G. Jung," *American Political Science Review* 67 (March 1973), p. 144.

58. Ibid.

59. C.G. Jung, *Symbols of Transformation*, trans. R.F.C. Hull, Bollingen Series 20 (Princeton: Princeton University Press, 1956), pp. 232, 228. Vol. 5.

60. Jacobi, *Complex/Archetype/Symbol*, p. 100.

61. C.G. Jung, *The Undiscovered Self*, trans. R.F.C. Hull (New York: Mentor Books, 1957), p. 96.

62. Ibid., p. 82.

63. Marcuse, *Eros and Civilization*, p. 219.

64. Edward Glover, *Freud or Jung?* (London: George Allen and Unwin Ltd., 1950), p. 168.

65. Ernest Jones, "The Theory of Symbolism" (amplified from a paper read before the British Psychological Society, January 29, 1916; published in the *British Journal of Psychology* 9, n.d.), in *Papers on Psychoanalysis* (London: Bailliere, Tindall and Cox, 1948), p. 117.

66. Marcuse, *Eros and Civilization*, p. 130.

67. Ibid., p. 128.

68. Ibid., p. 128.

69. Ibid., p. 129.

70. Ibid.

71. Ibid., p. 128.

72. Ibid., p. 154.

73. Ibid., p. 153.

74. Ibid., p. 154.

75. Ibid.

76. Ibid., p. 181.

77. Ibid., p. 133.

78. Ibid., p. 128.

79. Ibid., p. 144.

80. Carl G. Jung, *Psychological Types*, trans H. Godwin Baynes (New York: Harcourt, Brace and Company, Inc., 1926), p. 578.

81. Jack J. Spector, *The Aesthetics of Freud* (New York: Praeger Publishers, 1972), p. 101.

82. Ibid., p. 112.

83. Abraham Kaplan, "Freud and Modern Philosophy," in *Freud and*

the Twentieth Century, ed. Benjamin Nelson (London: George Allen and Unwin Ltd., 1958), p. 210.

84. Sigmund Freud, *Civilization and Its Discontents* (1929), trans, and ed. James Strachey (New York: W.W. Norton and Company Inc., 1961), p. 29.

85. Does Jung have the same attitude toward aesthetics that Freud does? Jung believes that culture has an autonomous existence, that it is not substitute gratification. However, in *Psychological Types*, he does state that "the aesthetic attitude shields one from being really concerned, from being personally implicated, which the religious understanding of the problem would entail" (p. 177). He makes a similar point when he argues that the aesthetic standpoint *"holds itself aloof from the problem"* (p. 178). These comments occur in his essay on Apollo and Dionysius. He argues that Nietzsche mistook a religious for an aesthetic problem: "Aestheticism can, of course, replace the religious function. But . . . it is none the less only a compensatory structure in a place of the real thing that is wanting. Moreover, Nietzsche's later 'conversion' to Dionysius shows very clearly that the aesthetic surrogate did not stand the test of time" (p. 176). Now granted, Jung and Marcuse appear to have a similar notion of aesthetics; however, Jung raises some interesting problems for Marcuse. The relationship between Marcuse's "private space" and Jung's "religious feeling" will be developed in a later chapter, as will the possibility of the concrete and lasting existence of an aesthetic alternative. Suffice it to say, for the purposes of this argument, both Jung and Marcuse can be said to believe that aesthetic relationships can provide models that are not connected to the existing modes of thought and perception, a belief not to be found in Freud.

86. Kaplan, "Freud and Modern Philosophy," in *Freud and the Twentieth Century*, p. 210.

87. C.G. Jung, *Collected Papers on Analytical Psychology* (London: Bailliere, Tindall and Cox, 1922), p. 468.

88. Ibid.

89. Marcuse, *Eros and Civilization*, p. 175.

90. Jung, *Collected Papers*, p. 181.

91. C.G. Jung, *Modern Man in Search of a Soul* (London: Kegan Paul, Trench, Trubner and Co. Ltd., 1933), pp. 186-87.

92. Ibid., pp. 198-99.

93. Ira Progoff, *Jung's Psychology and Its Social Meaning* (New York: Julian Press, Inc., 1953), p. 230.

94. Ibid., p. 186.

95. Leopold Stein, "What Is a Symbol Supposed to Be?" *Journal of Analytical Psychology* 2 (January 1957), p. 80.

CHAPTER 5

A Critical Examination of Marcuse's Vision: An Analysis of the Aesthetic As Therapeutic

Marcuse has been labeled a Marxist, but this description must be qualified. He is primarily concerned with those elements of Marx which indicate the importance of a change in consciousness. He expresses this concern directly in *Reason and Revolution:*

> Of course, the consciousness of men will continue to be determined by the material processes that reproduce their society, even when men have come to regulate their social relations in such a way that these contribute best to the free development of all. But when these material processes have been made rational and have become the conscious work of men, the blind dependence of consciousness on social conditions will cease to exist. Reason, when determined by rational social conditions, is determined by itself. Socialist freedom embraces both sides of the relation between consciousness and social existence.[1]

These changes in consciousness involve reintegration of repressed elements of human existence, found in what Marcuse calls the aesthetic dimension. A detailed examination of this concept will provide a more complete understanding of Marcuse's therapeutic vision.

Marcuse's vision of the aesthetic as therapeutic corresponds to Nietzsche's discussion of art in *The Birth of Tragedy*. In *The Birth of Tragedy*, Nietzsche, although he will abandon this contention, accepts a therapeutic function for political philosophy. Like Marcuse and Jung, his vision is one of reintegration, conceived of as a reactivation.

Nietzsche speaks of cultures as Socratic (Alexandrian), artistic (Hellenic), or tragic (Buddhistic). For Nietzsche, our culture is Alexandrian; it is dominated by "the Socratic love of knowledge and the delusion of being able thereby to heal the eternal world of existence."[2] The delusion is one of limitless power. There are, however, internal contradictions inherent in the Alexandrian culture. It requires a slave class, and the existence of this class gives rise to an inner disturbance related to the unrealized promise of equality for all. But this culture, in which consciousness is equivalent to reason and optimism is inherent in reason, lacks the means or the faith in the means to deal with these inner disturbances.

Nietzsche argues that religion, which has become permeated by the dominant culture, is "pale" and cannot handle the discontents emanating from the Alexandrian culture. Even the domain of myth has been invaded. The culture is frightened, and science no longer appears to have universal validity.

In *One-Dimensional Man*, Marcuse argues that one-dimensional society has eliminated man's private space:

> But the term "introjection" perhaps no longer describes the way in which the individual by himself reproduces and perpetuates the external controls exercised by his society. Introjection suggests a variety of relatively spontaneous processes by which a Self (Ego) transposes the "outer" into the "inner." Thus introjection implies the existence of an inner dimension distinguished from and even antagonistic to the external exigencies—an individual consciousness and an individual unconscious *apart from* public opinion and behavior. The idea of "inner freedom" here has its reality: it designates the private space in which man may become and remain "himself."
>
> Today this private space has been invaded and whittled down by technological reality. Mass production and mass distribution claim the *entire* individual, and industrial psychology has long ceased to be confined to the factory. The manifold processes of introjection seem to be ossified in almost mechanical reactions. The result is, not adjustment but *mimesis:* an immediate identification of the individual with *his* society and, through it, with the society as a whole.[3]

Jung sees religion as a force which cuts off the individual from dependence on the State. Religion, for Jung, represents man's relation to a dimension of existence other than the dominant mode of consciousness. Religion is a "dependence on and submission to the irrational facts of experience."[4] Religious convictions provide the individual with a transcedent inner experience which can protect him from submersion in the mass, the function Marcuse believes is performed by the aesthetic dimension. For Jung, man's religious feelings are important because they represent a non-social dimension, a realm of feeling which is in touch with the unconscious, an area that negates the total dependence on the State for definition. It is vital for Jung as well as Marcuse and Nietzsche to maintain a dimension apart from the dominant mode of existence of the given reality. Both Marcuse and Jung see this modern development as a recapitulation of (but not as a regression to) a former primitive mode of being. For Jung, the modern constitutional state begins to replicate the primitive community "where everybody is subject to the autocratic rule of a chief or an oligarchy."[5] For Marcuse, "This immediate automatic identification (which may have been characteristic of primitive forms of association) reappears in high industrial civilization."[6] Nietzsche concurs. He argues that art in the Alexandrian culture responds to what he calls a non-aesthetic need for the idyllic, for primordial existence.

Nietzsche, like Marcuse and Jung, has a therapeutic vision of regeneration which can stand in a healing relation to the diseased reality. In *Philosophy in the Tragic Age of the Greeks*, he abandons this view, a development traced by this study to his inadequate conception of symbol. Nietzsche, in *The Birth of Tragedy*, believes that it is possible to reawaken the Dionysian spirit, to liberate Art.

Like Marcuse, Nietzsche believes that true art is estranged from our culture and that this culture fears destruction by true art. Interestingly, this early Nietzsche, like Marcuse, bases his hopefulness to a large degree on the work of Kant:

Let us recollect further that Kant and Schopenhauer made it possible for *German philosophy*, streaming from similar sources, to destroy scientific Socratism's complacent delight in existence by establishing its boundaries; how through this delimitation was introduced an infinitely profounder and more serious view of ethical problems and of art, which we may designate as Dionysian wisdom comprised of concepts.[7]

Nietzsche, like Marcuse and Jung, believes not only that it is possible to tap a creative, therapeutic unconscious dimension, but that such an activity is necessary. Culture, Nietzsche argues, loses creativity when it loses myth to the dominant consciousness of a culture. Myth, he contends, keeps imagination from aimlessness. Nietzsche even argues that people who have experienced Dionysius can still exhibit patriotism and unity.

Nietzsche's indictment of the present culture is expressed in his discussion of Socrates. With Socrates, Nietzsche argues, the beautiful becomes linked with the intelligible. Socrates stands opposed to Dionysius. But Nietzsche's optimism is again apparent in his discussion of Socrates. He contends that the account of Socrates' last days might be an indication that he (Socrates) realized that there might be something other than what was intelligible to him, another realm of wisdom.

Nietzsche asks if the powers which opposed tragedy are strong enough to prevent the artistic reawakening. His answer, like Marcuse's, is an optimistic reaffirmation of the dialectic:

> If ancient tragedy was diverted from its course by the dialetical desire for knowledge and the optimism of science, this fact might lead us to believe that there is an eternal conflict between *the theoretic and the tragic world view*; and only after the spirit of science has been pursued to its limits, and its claim to universal validity destroyed by the evidence of these limits may we hope for a rebirth of tragedy—a form of culture for which we should have to use the symbol *of the music-practicing Socrates* in the sense spoken of above.[8]

Marcuse's aesthetic vision, like that of Nietzsche, attempts to reintegrate the Dionysian element. With Dionysius we are members of a higher community. Dionysius excites man's symbolic faculties. Nietzsche, like Marcuse, leads to a type of elitism; only a few are able to understand Dionysius. Nietzsche, again like Marcuse, uses symbols in his therapeutic vision. Nietzsche calls for a new world of symbols to express the totality of human power.

Art, for Nietzsche, develops from the Apollo-Dionysius duality. These two forces activate and incite one another. Nietzsche's aesthetic man uses images to interpret life. The realms of Apollo and Dionysius, for Nietzsche, appear to represent "truth" that, when brought to a culture as vital forces, can be therapeutic. Marcuse's aesthetic dimension is a realm of truth, a domain of objectivity and validity. He incorporates Nietzsche's theory of art as previously outlined and, as he so often does when attempting to work through a vital thesis, turns to Hegel and Kant for his strength. In *Counterrevolution and Revolt*, Marcuse attempts to contribute to Marxian aesthetics through a discussion of what has been commonly referred to as the "cultural revolution." Ironically, he begins his discussion of this "contribution" with what appears to be a direct repudiation of a fundamental orthodox Marxist tenet. In the chapter entitled "Art and Revolution," Marcuse contends that "Cultural changes can no longer be adequately understood within the abstract schema of base and superstructure (ideology)."[9]

For Marcuse, aesthetic values have a validity, an objectivity, a truth of their own. Marcuse's comments echo the language of Hegel and Kant: "The aesthetic representation of the Idea, of the universal in the particular, leads art to transform particular (historical) conditions into universal ones: to show as the tragic or cosmic fate of man what is only his fate in the established society."[10] For Marcuse, a work of art has objectivity. The aesthetic experience reveals what Marcuse would argue is the Hegelian universal as opposed to and above the particular historical experience and also responds to certain "constant qualities of the human intellect, sensibility, and imagination—qualities which the tradition of philosophical aesthetics has interpreted as the idea of beauty."[11] It is the Form which makes a work into a work of art, for "by virtue of the Form, and the Form alone, the content achieves that uniqueness which makes it the content of one particular work of art and no other."[12] The realm of Forms, for Marcuse, is an historical reality. The Form is that "which distinguishes Art from any other product of human activity."[13] The Form can act on human behavior because it is the Form which will provide the model for the New Sensibility.

In *Eros and Civilization*, Marcuse discusses Kant's concept of aesthetic function. Again, what is interesting is not so much whether or not Marcuse correctly reads Kant, but what he expects or claims to find in Kant. What he expects, and this is vital to Marcuse's conception of the aesthetic dimension, is the link among pleasure, beauty, freedom, and autonomy. Marcuse's own symbols of Orpheus and Narcissus attempt to communicate the potential erotic union of man and nature, "where order is beauty and work is play."[14] Marcuse argues that there was a time when the original psychic energy was undifferentiated; Eros and Thantos in their present form are, for Marcuse, historical modifications of this original unity. Marcuse sees in Kant a theoretical explanation for his notion of aesthetic objectivity: "Although sensuous and therefore receptive, the aesthetic imagination is creative: in a free synthesis of its own, it constituted *beauty*. In the aesthetic imagination, sensuousness generates universally valid principles for an objective order."[15]

Why are objectivity and validity so important for Marcuse's conception of an aesthetic dimension? In "Repressive Tolerance," Marcuse argues that art stands opposed to history and subjects reality to different laws. These are the laws of the Form and are the negation of the existing reality. Art is subjected to history when it enters the struggle with history, for history enters into art's definition.[16] Again, it is in Kant that Marcuse sees the link between sensuousness and the aesthetic dimension: "This pleasure derives from the perception of the pure *form* of an object, regardless of its 'matter' and of its (internal or external) 'purpose.' "[17] He sees in Kant the outline of therapeutic regeneration. The aesthetic faculty mediates between sensuousness and reason, reconciling these spheres of human existence which have become separated. The aesthetic state must defeat the course of time; it must harmonize man and nature, the objective and the subjective world. This is why the aesthetic dimension must have objectivity and validity; it must remain autonomous from the existing society, or it will be without force in the face of the dominant mode of consciousness. It becomes the role of the intellectual to open the mental space for the liberation of society, to recall the historical possibilities which have become known as utopian possibilities in the struggle against the dominant reality.[18] Freedom, or the struggle to attain freedom, becomes linked to education or progress in the development of a consciousness of freedom. The self can become more than a reflection of the society in which it exists.

Marcuse is aware that the reality can swallow up the protest element in art. The existing reality can, however, be strengthened by this co-optation by diverting opposition to personal and private rebellion and away from public political opposition. Marcuse believes that it is objectivity and validity which can give the aesthetic dimension the power to withstand absorption and to retain a transcendent relation. Jung can give Marcuse this objectivity. Jung's collective unconscious, like Marcuse's aesthetic dimension, does not depend for its power on consciousness but can stand in a positive dialectical therapeutic relationship to consciousness. Jung's symbols have a content that goes beyond reflections of consciousness, which can heal and stand in the relationshop to the diseased reality that Marcuse desires for Orpheus and Narcissus.

There are certain difficulties with Marcuse's theory. Hauser, a writer in the tradition of aesthetic criticism, raises critical points applicable to Marcuse. Marcuse is not an aesthetic theoretician per se and as such cannot be expected to present a detailed analysis of the nature and function of art. Although Hauser's work deals directly with art history, it can be related to Marcuse's discussion of the aesthetic dimension and, by extension, to the therapeutic function of political philosophy.

Hauser argues that the scientific treatment of art can destroy the aesthetic experience.[19] To recognize a therapeutic function of political philosophy is to recognize a non-conscious dimension of human experience. Since this dimension is non-conscious, it cannot be understood solely by cognitive reason. It is proper, however, to ask if this non-conscious domain of existence is the proper focus of political philosophy. Surely, it can be argued, if we are concerned with political matters, then we are concerned with public and therefore conscious matters. But if we accept the diagnoses of Marcuse, Jung, and Nietzsche, we must conclude that the therapeutic relationship or that which will heal the diseased reality cannot come solely from consciousness. What will be therapeutic are those elements which have remained untouched or free from consciousness. The ability to tap these elements cannot be restricted to cognitive thought.

Hauser puts into question the entire conception of aesthetic objectivity and validity. Marx, as Marcuse is aware, is concerned with this problem.[20] In *A Contribution to the Critique of Political Economy*, Marx puzzles as to why, if they are associated with certain forms of social development, Greek art and epic poetry can still give aesthetic pleasure. Marcuse rejects Marx's explanation that we stand in relation to this work in the same way as we stand in relation to the charms of our childhood. Marcuse is much more interested in what he believes to be Marx's recognition of some transcendent element in art: "As regards art, it is well known that some of its peaks by no means correspond to the general development of society; nor do they therefore to the material sub-structure, the skeleton as it were of its organization."[21] Marcuse does not see artistic creation as a reflection of the base. Aesthetic values for him have a timelessness and a universality. Hauser argues that artistic creations are more closely linked with the time in which they are created than with the "idea of art in general or the history of art as a unitary process."[22] Hauser seems to think that Marx, in the *Critique of Political Economy*, believed in some kind of timeless validity, supporting but not validating Marcuse's interpretation. Hauser's comments on aesthetic validity are par-ticularly pointed when considering Marcuse's aesthetics. The theory of validity, Hauser argues, was a reaction against scien-tific positivism. He traces this theory to Plato's reaction to the Sophists. This resulted in the conception of spiritual qualities hav-ing an independent structure. The spiritual realm was autonomous. True statements have objectivity. Validity is taken to be separate from approval or acceptance, which are historically, psycho-logically, or in some way empirically conditioned. Furthermore, Hauser believes that: "from this objective and normative character of values, the theory of validity tacitly infers their timelessness; as values appear to be superindividual, they come to be represented by it as superhistorical."[23] Hauser argues that this theory confuses objectivity with timelessness. What he calls a significant structure, value, or standard can be separable from the causal conditions of its origin but still historically modified. This point is important because Marcuse's vision proposes to refute time. Hauser contends that all valid truths and acknowledged values are not emanations from a world of forms but, rather, are human creations. He proposes that if the term *validity* is to be used with art, it can only be used with already realized values, not absolute eternal values that can be "realized" by the artist. Hauser attacks the very source of the power of Marcuse's aesthetic dimension. He argues that works of art do not derive their effectiveness from any sort of "Form" but rather from the fact that they respond to actual, historically conditioned requirements.

This criticism is closely related to what could be considered a Freudian criticism of Marcuse's aesthetics. Hauser can elaborate this criticism. Freud presents perhaps the most devastating attack on a transcendent conception of aesthetics. As Hauser reads Freud, the artist is concerned only indirectly with Form and beauty; he does not aim for beauty but for a means to defend against life's problems. Beauty becomes the artist's tool to confront reality. Freud's conception of aesthetics, like his conception of symbol and fantasy discussed earlier, is in effect opposed to Marcuse. On the other hand, although Jung speaks more in terms of a religious rather than an aesthetic therapy, Jung's conception of aesthetics—particularly the visionary mode—is compatible with Marcuse.

Jung, Marcuse, and Nietzsche appear to link artistic creation to a transcendent, autonomous, unconscious dimension. Hauser, on the contrary, feels that the conscious element in artistic creation dominates the unconscious. Hauser would contend that the aesthetic dimension is not the proper domain of the political philosopher, for he argues that the process of artistic creation is conscious and therefore not suitable subject matter for depth psychology.

The preceding discussion leads to perhaps the most devastating criticism of Marcuse's aesthetic theory. Marcuse's therapeutic vision, it could be argued, may be a mystification of reality, the substitution of a veil of harmony and unity for the actual contradictions of concrete, historical existence. Hauser reasons that all art has the element of illusion, of the daydream, of (it is possible to imply) the mystification of reality. Nietzsche was aware of this Apollonian aspect of art, and Marcuse details how a one-sided Apollonian reality can become a perverted world of universals. Hauser, however, contends that all attempts to "schematize" history (including dialectics) are philosophical mysticism. He argues that art is a language but not a language of primal man or an anterior mode of expression intelligible by all. He says that art would be useless as a means of communication if it "relied on some ad hoc means of expression."[24] Hauser implies that if art met all of Marcuse's criteria, it would be ineffective:

> Spontaneity by itself cannot produce anything communicable or comprehensible. A work of art that consisted entirely of original, strictly creative elements would be unintelligible; it becomes intelligible only through a sacrifice of originality. The living, pre-rational experience of the individual must first undergo a certain rationalization and conventionalization if it is to emerge from the purely private sphere and carry some of its meaning into the world of interpersonal relations.[25]

Marcuse would argue that his vision of reintegration is not "spontaneous" in this sense. His vision, as noted when Parekh's criticisms were discussed, emerges out of and against the concrete historical process. Marcuse argues that it is imperative to find means of communicating liberating potentialities.[26] If political philosophy is to be therapeutic, it cannot confine itself to conscious concerns. Cognitive thought alone cannot express these liberating potentialities. Perhaps this inability to communicate these potentialities, foreseen in *The Birth of Tragedy*, accounts in some part for Nietzsche's later pessimism:

> Language can never adequately render the cosmic symbolism of music, because music stands in symbolic relation to the primordial contradiction and primordial pain in the heart of the primal unity, and therefore symbolizes a sphere which is beyond and prior to all phenomena. Rather, all phenomena, compared with it, are merely *symbols*: hence *language*, as the organ and symbol of phenomena, can never by any means disclose the innermost heart of music; language, in its attempt to imitate it, can only be in superficial contact with music; while all the eloquence of lyric poetry cannot bring the deepest significance of the latter one step nearer to us.[27]

Marcuse all but ignores the possible pathological effects of his call for a New Sensibility, but he does list possible objections to his aesthetic theory.[28] However, Marcuse is safe in offering these as possible criticisms, for he has dealt with all of them in the course of his collected works. Naturally, this does not imply that Marcuse has *successfully* resolved these suggested problems, but he also has not been unaware of them. Marcuse notes, as a possible criticism of aesthetic theory, the idea that the whole notion of "aesthetic" theory doesn't adequately express the real human condition. This, of course, is the opposite of one of Marcuse's own direct contentions. As he has stated repeatedly, it is the present-day consciousness (including contemporary philosophy) which fails to take into account the whole range of human existence. Aesthetic theory, he argues, reunites sensuousness and reason through a therapeutic process involving new perceptual syntheses.

Marcuse also speaks to the objection that aesthetic theory creates a world of illusion and is divorced from reality—one of the problems Hauser suggests. Marcuse counters that it is the tension between art and reality which is responsible for the potential therapeutic energy art can generate. Marcuse is aware that to make art part of reality is to make art into pseudo-art. Art can never be a substitute for reality, but it can provide models to heal reality. These models are incorporated into the New Sensibility, which in turn provides new, reintegrated structures for thought and perception. Again there is some question of the nature of Marcuse's conception of the domain of art, of the Form. Marcuse has asserted that this is an historical reality, yet it is supposedly outside of and stands opposed to history. He appears to be arguing that art does not represent the work of the Spirit but is a concrete historical manifestation which has resisted the Performance Principle. Concerning the objection that sensuousness is repressed in the illusion created by art, Marcuse has argued—referring to Kant— that sensuousness and reason are united in the aesthetic mode. He contends that repressive desublimation is not in the service of Eros but instead diffuses Eros and concentrates it in sexuality, which can be given free reign since it is ineffectual in this diffused form. This logic enables him to counter what he considers to be the fourth objection to his aesthetic theory, that the aesthetic form stabilizes reality and is repressive. Marcuse has discussed this possibility with his comments on affirmative culture; and has argued that true art is never absorbed by or supportive of reality but stands in negation to it, containing the possibility of liberation.

As has been noted, Marcuse has at least attempted to deal with the objections he does list. What is interesting, however, is that

Marcuse does (in *Counterrevolution and Revolt*) cite a piece which offers certain other possible objections with which, for some reason or other, he does not elect to deal. It is worthwhile to examine some of these points contained in Edgar Wind's *Art and Anarchy*.

Wind argues that the imaginative forces have potentially disruptive powers and that the artist must deal economically with these. Overindulgence, he continues, will destroy by excess. He lists others who are aware of this danger, who hold what he calls this "sacred fear": Plato, Goethe, and Baudelaire. Plato, Wind argues, believed that man could be transformed by what he imagined. He summarizes what he believes to be Plato's reasoning on this point:

> If the Greeks had not been so responsive to an exquisite phrase or a beautiful gesture, they might have judged a political oration by its truth and not by the splendour with which it was delivered: but their sobriety was undermined by their imagination.[29]

The development of Nietzsche's work could be offered as a possible historical example of this possibility, of the pathological effects of an unleashed Dionysius. Clegg, in an article on Freud and the Homeric mind, discusses the same possibility that Wind suggests.

Clegg attempts to trace Freud's debt to Nietzsche. In the course of his analysis he summarizes what has already been discussed as Freud's critique of Marcuse's theory of aesthetics. In Clegg's terms:

> Since the poet and his hero are the same in their mentality, Freud's position amounts to a description of the artist as the licensed barbarian in our midst who can never adjust to the painful, but necessary and ultimately rewarding, demands of culture.[30]

The artist for Freud is only compensating for "cultural ineptitudes."

> Unfit to be raised from a state of nature by the acquisition of compensatory knowledge, he can—when finding himself housed against his will in a state of culture—only seek a differing, unteachable kind of compen-

sation by turning to the arts which allow him to revert to an irrational, unfettered existence.[31]

Plato, argues Clegg, was aware of the possible dangerous existence of the artist and his antisocial appetites. Furthermore, Clegg believes that Freud reinstates Plato's indictment of art.

Wind cites Jacob Burckhardt's book, *The Civilization of the Renaissance*, as further evidence of the possible connection between aesthetic forms and political disintegration. Wind states that "in the Italian Renaissance, again, the most splendid release of artistic energies was attended by political disintegration."[32] Wind also mentions, in this context, Hegel's comments on the disintegration of Athens. It is worthwhile to examine Hegel's ideas on this point in more detail. Marcuse relies quite heavily upon Hegel for a resolution of what can be called the *principium individuationis* problem but seems oblivious to these observations of Hegel which present problems for his argument.

Hegel argues, in the *Philosophy of History*, that it was subjective freedom which was the destructive element for the Greeks.[33] The Athenian culture was directed toward realizing the Beautiful. The Greeks occupied what Hegel calls the middle ground of Beauty, not Truth. By this, Hegel means that the Greeks lacked spiritual self-consciousness. There was no emancipation from the natural element, no emancipation from immediacy. The ethics were personal; what was regarded as right or moral lacked confirmation in terms of reflection on the presence of the Spirit. As Hegel puts it, the aesthetic culture cannot be the final resting place of the Spirit. The corruption comes from this subjective morality and system of ethics. This is why the golden age lasted only about sixty years (492 B.C. to 431 B.C.). The "germ of corruption" came from the principle of subjectivity which is inevitable in a culture of beauty. Subjectivity is characterized by primitive, unreflecting immediacy. The Greeks lacked an abstract principle of Truth and Virtue. In its stead they developed a basis of morality in the individual, and this subjectivity became the key for decisions which resulted in corruption and disintegration.

It is only possible to infer Marcuse's answer to this. He argues that man has an innate moral structure and that the values he is calling for to be reintegrated from the aesthetic dimension have objectivity and universality. Here again, a synthesis with Jung can strengthen Marcuse's argument in the face of Hegel's objection. The collective unconscious is the domain of objectivity and universality. A therapeutic reintegration of the collective unconscious would not drown the individual in a sea of subjectivity because the psyche is objective. In the terms of the argument presented in this study, a culture which undergoes a therapeutic feminization would be grounded on an innate, objective morality and would not fall victim to the subjectivity that destroyed Athens. For Hegel, Athens's glory was brief because it was based on the Beautiful rather than on the Spirit. The Greeks, he argued, lacked self-conscious reflection; that is, they were not emancipated from what he calls the natural element. Athens became the victim of subjectivity because objectivity can come only through reflection of the Spirit.

A therapeutic feminization taps an objective dimension; the individual and society, in Marcuse's aesthetic vision, would not be victims of Athenian subjectivity. The individual personal ethics that Hegel saw as a cause of Athens's decline would be replaced by an objective morality rooted in the human psyche. It is only when the individuals are separated and not bound to a community that subjectivity becomes disastrous.

Wind argues that we share with the artist the threat of the imaginative forces. As such, we should take precautions, or we will be overwhelmed by these forces. Wind contends that Hegel realized that when art is taken to a "zone of safety," it will no longer effect our existence. Plato, reasons Wind, did not realize that people could become immune to the dangers of art. Hegel, on the other hand, believed that art would always remain "disengaged from reality." Wind's argument merits a closer examination. Marcuse, as can be seen from Wind's own words, uses aspects of Hegel which support his argument but selectively ignores those elements in Hegel which present a problem for his argument:

Plato did not foresee that the dangers of art, which he feared so greatly, might not affect a people who had become immune to them. Hegel, on the contrary, could not imagine that art would ever again become dangerous. Although he envisaged an art of the future which might be richer and subtler than the art he had seen, he supposed that, no matter how varied our art might become, it would always remain disengaged from reality because, as he put it, "art has worked itself out." According to Hegel, when art becomes pure it ceases to be serious, and in that consists its final splendour.[34]

Quite obviously, Hegel, in Marcuse's terms, no longer sees any potential pathological effects of art because of the development of what is known as the "affirmative character" of culture. However, Marcuse believes that the dialectic will shatter this affirmative character. Marcuse is presented with this dilemma: Hegel argues that objectivity depends upon the diffusion of the power of art, but Marcuse contends that it is the reactivation of art and the aesthetic dimension which must precede the development of a new, objective Sensibility. If Hegel is correct, and Marcuse so often believes him to be, then Marcuse's therapeutic vision actually involves the opening of a Pandora's box of subjectivity and relativity which will result in corruption and disintegration. Marcuse apparently ignores this element of Hegel. Marcuse's therapeutic vision, when considered in light of this Hegelian objection, would be pathological rather than therapeutic.

Now, it has been argued that a synthesis with Jung can resolve some of these problems associated with subjectivity and the aesthetic dimension. However, this synthesis itself brings another problem to the argument. Odajnyk, in an article which discusses Jung's political philosophy, notes possible pathological phenomena resulting from the assimilation of contents of the collective unconscious. Odajnyk speaks of many forms of this phenomena but subsumes them under the general Jungian term *psychic inflation*, which involves the extension of the personality beyond individual limits. This can be pathological because it can involve the overwhelming of the ego by the mana quality of the archetypes. The ego may feel that it masters the archetype, but the archetype is the actual master of the ego.[35] Psychic inflation can appear in collective form. This phenomenon can lead to political tyranny or rebellion, depending on the extent and type of the population's identification with the political leader. Basically, psychic inflation can introduce an irrational, uncontrollable element into political considerations. The collective unconscious, which can never be known directly, can, as Jung recognizes, become dominant in the psyche. However, this study has always stressed the Jungian position in this regard. It is worth repeating: the psyche is only dangerous if ignored. To say that there is a danger in Marcuse's therapeutic vision and that, therefore, the vision should be discredited is to open the path for a potentially more dangerous alternative, the assumption that human nature is one-dimensional and that political considerations should be confined to conscious concerns.

The comparison of Marcuse's and Nietzsche's aesthetic theories reveals that Marcuse's ideas are not unique in an ahistorical sense but represent a dynamic development of some of the major ideas in the tradition of Western thought.

As has been noted frequently throughout this study, Marcuse often turns to Hegel for the resolution of problems he comes upon in the course of the development of his ideas. What is interesting is that Marcuse appears to ignore Hegel's discussion of the decline of the golden years of Athens. This particular section of Hegel would appear to speak to the heart of Marcuse's conception of the aesthetic as therapeutic; yet, Marcuse ignores Hegel's contention that a culture based on Beauty cannot endure, that Beauty can never be the final resting place of the Spirit. Marcuse's aesthetic theory as such is subject to many of the criticisms leveled against what can be referred to as classical aesthetic theory. However, Hegel's observations themselves may well prove to be the most telling criticisms of Marcuse's vision.

Is Marcuse actually an original thinker in a dialectical sense; or is he, more accurately, an eclectic thinker who has failed to resolve the contradictions inherent in his own work? This question is perhaps the most significant that can be asked of Marcuse when attempting to evaluate the contributions he can make to political philosophy.

In effect, this study has become an attempt to construct, through a synthesis of Marcuse and Jung, a new paradigm for political philosophy. The term *therapeutic function* has been employed in recognition that political philosophy can and does have many functions, one of which is the therapeutic. As such, this approach does not claim exclusivity; nevertheless, it is subject to many of the pitfalls surrounding paradigm construction. Skinner lucidly outlines these dangers in an article in *History and Theory*[36]

Skinner labels these dangers "mythologies." In particular, he warns a reader may expect to find comments on a certain subject in a text and then attempt to arrange what are actually random comments on a subject into some type of organized doctrine. This "mythology" may give rise to the absurd situation of faulting an author for the failure to discuss, or discuss thoroughly enough, this "doctrine" which actually exists only in the reader's preconceived mental set.

Marcuse, as has been noted, explicitly rejects Jung. Such terms like *therapeutic* and *vision* are not Marcuse's. Isn't this study, in effect, guilty of "mythology?" It is to be hoped that enough evidence has been presented throughout the course of this study to convince the reader that Marcuse does recognize a therapeutic function for political philosophy. More directly, the attempted synthesis between Marcuse and Jung would appear to be susceptible to Skinner's objections. Marcuse himself may well resolve this difficulty. He is an original thinker in a dialectical sense; his work involves syntheses of ideas and concepts. The reason why Marcuse rejects Jung may remain a mystery; however, this study has attempted to demonstrate that a synthesis with Jung can revitalize both Marcuse's thought and the therapeutic function of political philosophy.

There are other difficulties, beyond those suggested by Skinner, both with the notion of a therapeutic function for political philosophy and with the approach used in this study. This approach urges the inclusion of an unconscious dimension into the domain of political philosophy. The vision of the political philosopher functions to tap the unconscious dimension. The contents of the collective unconscious are objective and universal; and, through their reintegration, the therapeutic vision can revitalize consciousness. Marcuse is aware of this therapeutic function of political philosophy; he argues that fantasy must not be excluded from philosophy, for it is fantasy which retains the link to the unconscious dimension. However, the inclusion of this unconscious dimension is not free of problems. It could be argued that our advances, both in the discipline of political "science" and in modern industrial society, have come about as a result of the victory of "rationality." The political philosopher, it has been argued, in the attempt to tap the unconscious dimension would lift man out of what Eliade calls profane time and into the realm of sacred time. The therapeutic vision of the political philosopher involves the negation of time as that which binds man to repression and domination. Altizer attacks this entire notion of the recapitulation, at a later stage, of Eliade's primitive form of unity.

Modern man's alienation, Altizer argues, involves the separation of man from the cosmos and the sacred from reality. We cannot know, he contends, an integrated existence or a sacred Reality. Our condition is wholly and totally profane. We have chosen autonomous freedom; as such, we have precluded the sacred and the transcendent. Altizer conceives of human existence in Sartre's sense: "Modern man becomes himself by a process of desacralization: as Nietzsche saw, he must become the murderer of God."[37] Desacralization is a requirement for autonomy; religion can be only a human and historical phenomenon. To use myth is to turn away from concrete existence: "The sacred can be actualized only by means of a dissolution or sublimation of profane existence."[38]

Altizer's argument is not incompatible with Marcuse's vision. Marcuse contends that we must go to a new continuum, from quantitative to qualitative progress. Although the possibilities for transcendence come about as consequences of historical actualities developed in concrete existence, the process can go into a new dimension which is at the same time the negation and the fulfillment of these historical potentialities. For Altizer, the actualization of mythical modes of being can come about only as a result of the dissolution of existing categories of perception and experience. This is, in effect, the purpose of Marcuse's call for a New Sensibility. He would negate the old categories of perception, experience, and thought (including space and time) which perpetuate repression and domination.

However, Marcuse leaves unanswered some very difficult questions. Nowhere does he deal in any detail with the questions of whether or not the approximation of mythical unity and existence can exist or correlate with the demands of modern industrial society or whether the institution of new perceptual and conceptual paradigms can maintain and sustain the advanced technical base. This study, too, has dealt offhandedly with these important considerations. Again, the only justification is the question of focus. The main concern of this study has been the therapeutic function of political philosophy and the demonstration of the possibility of the revitalization of this function through a synthesis of Marcuse and Jung. The questions which have been raised at this later stage are not to be dismissed; they can provide still further grounds for future work.

Tudor, in a perceptive book on political myths, raises additional objections to the inclusion of mythical modes of being in a discussion of a therapeutic vision of a non-repressive reality. Tudor brings into question the very definition of myth used in this study. He criticizes some of Gunnell's formulations, which were discussed in earlier chapters. Gunnell, Tudor argues, misuses history by taking isolated features of archaic culture and making them into a world view. For Tudor, there are myths in which the sacred plays no role; and, he contends, most modern political myths are in this category. Again, this particular criticism is easily answered by Marcuse. He would argue that political language, as it now appears in one-dimensional society, does use Tudor's more narrow definition of myth as a story about actual events and people. However, Marcuse could contend, Tudor does not preclude another conception of myth, for Tudor argues that a myth is "a device men adopt in order to come to grips with reality."[39] Tudor has contended that Eliade has arbitrarily defined myth in terms of relation to the sacred. Although Tudor reasons that most political myths do not speak to the presence of sacred realities, he does admit that this is a possible subject matter for myth. In effect, Tudor objects to Gunnell's and Eliade's selection of a single aspect of primitive man's existence and the elevation of this aspect to a mode of existence. Even if Tudor's objections are valid, they do not preclude Gunnell's and Eliade's formulations. Tudor does contend that myths function to bring order out of chaos. This is important to the political philsopher's vision. Marcuse argues that his vision of a non-repressive reality is material and historical, that it arises out of man's potential. To argue that the vision involves a recapitulation of a primitive mode of being is to argue that there is evidence in man's existence that he is capable of a different mode of being. This is not to argue that Marcuse would replace contemporary with primitive modes of being. Such a change, for Marcuse, would be a mystification of reality. Marcuse is aware of the demands of a technical society; and, cognizant of these demands, he argues for a dialectical advancement to a New Sensibility which contains this previous mode of non-repressive existence.

These objections in themselves, however, suggest another problem for this conception of a therapeutic function for political philosophy. To argue that the political philosopher can stand in a therapeutic relationship to the existing reality and, through his vision, which involves the negation of time, "heal" this reality might imply the devaluation of the material mode of existence. The therapeutic vision, since it must negate time, can be considered as devaluing what is defined by time, material existence.

Marcuse, like Arendt in *The Human Condition*, argues for a separate private sphere of existence. It can be seen from a comparison of Marcuse and Arendt that Marcuse, unlike Arendt, does not devalue by separating this private dimension. For Arendt, the condition of modern man is characterized by a dissolution of separate private and public realms. She sees the emergence of the social realm as a modern phenomenon. The social realm, she contends, is neither public nor private; it is a form in which survival activities appear in public and what is necessary for life assumes public significance.[40] Arendt contends that the image of the polis wasn't bound to scarcity; the necessities of life were obtained in private, a condition for freedom in the polis. She argues that the need for others is not fundamentally human. What is fundamentally human for Arendt is the capacity for political organization.

Marcuse realizes that it is necessary to maintain a separate private realm, but he proposes a different function for this realm. For Marcuse, the private is not the hiding place of the particular or the individual; it is the domain of opposition to the existing society. Then, it is appropriate to ask, is Marcuse actually a "political" philosopher?

R.N. Berki appears to speak to this question. In an article in the *Journal of Politics*, he argues that it is possible to identify two separate strains in the tradition of radical thought, the religious and the political. The religious, in Berki's terms, has to do with "thought and activity primarily concerned with the *inner*, the intra-human dimension."[41] In contrast, the political is concerned with "the *outer*, the 'public realm,' the inter-human dimension."[42] These strains are potentially contradictory, and it is this possibility which

Berki believes is realized in Marcuse's thought. Berki presents Marcuse as the "thinker in whose doctrine the political and religious strains of radical thought are set on a spectacular collision course."[43] Berki contends that Marcuse's emphasis on spiritual and moral problems renders his thought ineffective in dealing with political problems.

Berki has fundamentally erred in his interpretation of Marcuse. Rather than suffering from a confusion of the private and public, Marcuse's theory asserts that a primary symptom and/or cause of society's illness is the obliteration of the distance between the private and the public realms. He argues that this mimesis of public and private, of individual and society in modern industrial civilization, fails to provide the autonomy that freedom requires. It would appear, although this is not clear in Marcuse, that the individual would always remain in an antagonistic relationship to society. A healthy society could be inhabited by healthy people; a non-repressive society would be characterized by harmony between individual and societal needs.

Marcuse is a political philosopher in the most fundamental sense. His vision would symbolically order reality. Marcuse's vision, however, can itself be repressive. This is why a synthesis with Jung is so important both for Marcuse and for a therapeutic function for political philosophy. For too long, the political, in its attempts to order reality, has imposed a repressive order on this reality. A synthesis with Jung can open the way for what has been referred to in this study as the "feminization" of political thought and of concrete reality.

It could be argued that political philosophy should more properly be concerned with the "de-mythologizing" of reality, with the subjection of reality to conscious elaboration. The conception of the political as a symbolic ordering can result in repression of the unconscious dimension of human existence. This is why the synthesis of Marcuse and Jung was offered. Still, any discussion of man's symbolic faculty must take note of possible dangers. It has been demonstrated that man, when employing his symbolic faculty to order his reality, has constructed a political dimension which can repress the unconscious dimension. Edelman is aware of the intricacies of this dilemma.

Man's symbolic faculties, Edelman argues, enable him to engage in complex reasoning, planning, and effective action; however, this same ability can subject him to illusions, misperceptions, and self-defeating action. This is man's Janus-faced condition; the faculty which strengthens him and enables him to stand in an active relationship to the world and his own existence can also preclude effective action and deny his autonomous abilities. To study this symbolic faculty, then, is to study that which represents man's relationship to himself, others, and the world—to study, in effect, man's political relationships. Symbols enable man to perceive and organize the world. For Edelman, political cues specifically serve as "symbols of the whole." He argues that political symbols are unifying symbols; they can function in a way that individuals or groups seldom can. Edelman contends that myth, as a form of symbol, can create an identity among the masses which promotes "submissiveness and docility in the face of deprivation."[44] He offers the example of America's poor since the Civil War to demonstrate the potentially stultifying function of myth. Myths can subject masses to still other dangers, the depiction of Manichaean struggles or stratified social orders which preclude mobility. Certain feelings like anger and acquiescence can arise contrary to creativity. These myth-related feelings can inhibit "search and flexibility"; the myth can trap people and keep them committed to it even when it weakens rather than strengthens them. Banality and/or fear can result. The holder of the myth can become like Sartre's anti-Semite, trapped in an irrational web of fear and aggression which can be dealt with only by directing it outwardly to another person or group of persons. The introduction of the discussion of these unconscious elements into the language of political discourse may reinforce tendencies toward primitive modes of thought and may be pathological in and for modern industrial society. In effect, this attempt to introduce metaphoric and symbolic elements into the language of political discourse may reinforce irrationality. As Edelman notes, language doesn't create but rather mirrors reality. He argues the following:

In their polar forms the myths make the world meaningful and rationalize the conformity for those least able to assert, express, and identify themselves through innovative behavior or demonstrated political efficacy. They catalyze uncritical attachment to established leaders, regardless of the particular policies they pursue.[45]

However, Edelman—even with the recognition of these potential dangers—concurs with Jung; the unconscious dimension cannot be ignored. As he so vividly describes it: "Political analysis is ultimately adequate and enlightening in the measure that it takes full account of man's complexity and of his potentialities."[46]

To say that Edelman concurs with Jung is not to reach a conclusion or resolve a problem. There still remains the possibility of pathological effects which may be inherent to the inclusion of symbolic elements in the language of political discourse. Symbols can become meaningless to the individual and the community; that is, they can lose their affective power to transform and assimilate unconscious contents. Symbols can be manipulated by leaders to the detriment of the individual and the community.[47] They can also create an illusion of community and harmony; people can be led to believe they accept the same thing for the same reason when, in reality, the reasons behind their acceptances differ. Even in light of these objections, however, it is appropriate to once again reiterate a major thesis of this study: to deny or choose to deny or ignore the existence of the unconscious dimension does not lessen its influence. As Jung has noted, it is this attitude which accentuates the "danger" of the unconscious.

NOTES

1. Marcuse, *Reason and Revolution*, pp. 319-20.
2. Nietzsche, *The Birth of Tragedy*, p. 109.
3. Marcuse, *One-Dimensional Man*, p. 10.
4. Jung, *The Undiscovered Self*, p. 29.
5. Ibid., p. 27.
6. Marcuse, *One-Dimensional Man*, p. 10.
7. Nietzsche, *Birth of Tragedy*, pp. 120-21.
8. Ibid., p. 106.
9. Marcuse, *Counterrevolution and Revolt*, p. 82.
10. Ibid., p. 108.
11. Ibid., p. 87.

12. Herbert Marcuse, "Art as a Form of Reality," in *On the Future of Art*, sponsored by the Solomon R. Guggenheim Museum (New York: Viking Press, 1970), p. 126.

13. Ibid.

14. Marcuse, *Eros and Civilization*, p. 160.

15. Ibid., pp. 161-62.

16. Herbert Marcuse, "Repressive Tolerance," in *A Critique of Pure Tolerance*, ed. Robert Paul Wolff, Barrington Moore, Jr., and Herbert Marcuse (Boston: Beacon Press, 1965), p. 89.

17. Marcuse, *Eros and Civilization*, p. 161.

18. Marcuse, "Repressive Tolerance," in *A Critique of Pure Tolerance*, pp. 81-82.

19. Arnold Hauser, *The Philosophy of Art History* (New York: Alfred A. Knopf, 1959), p. 13.

20. Marcuse, *Counterrevolution and Revolt*, p. 87.

21. Karl Marx, *A Contribution to the Critique of Political Economy*, trans S.W. Ryazanskaya, ed. Maurice Dobb (New York: International Publishers, New World Paperbacks, 1970), p. 215.

22. Hauser, *Philosophy of Art History*, p. 36.

23. Ibid., p. 168.

24. Ibid., p. 370.

25. Ibid., p. 371.

26. Marcuse, *Counterrevolution and Revolt*, p. 79.

27. Nietzsche, *Birth of Tragedy*, pp. 55-56.

28. Marcuse, *Counterrevolution and Revolt*, p. 91.

29. Edgar Wind, *Art and Anarchy* (New York: Random House, Vintage Books, 1969), p. 6.

30. Jerry S. Clegg, "Freud and the Homeric' Mind," *Inquiry* 17 (Winter 1974), p. 452.

31. Ibid., p. 453.

32. Wind, *Art and Anarchy*, p. 6.

33. G.W.F. Hegel, *Philosophy of History*, trans. J. Sibree (New York: P.F. Collier and Sons, 1901), p. 333.

34. Wind, *Art and Anarchy*, p. 15.

35. Odajnyk, "The Political Ideas of C.G. Jung," p. 150.

36. Quentin Skinner, "Meaning and Understanding in the History of Ideas," *History and Theory* 8 (November 1969).

37. Thomas J.J. Altizer, "The Religious Meaning of Myth and Symbol," in *Truth, Myth, and Symbol*, ed. Thomas J.J. Altizer, William A. Beardslee, and J. Harvey Young (Englewood Cliffs, N.J.: Prentice-Hall, Inc., 1962), pp. 91-92.

38. Ibid., p. 93.

39. Henry Tudor, *Political Myth* (New York: Praeger Publishers, 1972), p. 17.

40. Hannah Arendt, *The Human Condition* (Chicago: University of Chicago Press, 1958), p. 46.

41. R.N. Berki, "Marcuse and the Crisis of the New Radicalism: From Politics to Religion?" *Journal of Politics* 34 (February 1972), p. 59.

42. Ibid.

43. Ibid., p. 58.

44. Murray Edelman, *Politics as Symbolic Action* (Chicago: Markham Publishing Co., 1971), p. 55.

45. Ibid., p. 79.

46. Ibid., p. 172.

47. Gregor Sebba, "Symbol and Myth in Modern Rationalistic Societies," in *Truth, Myth, and Symbol*, p. 150.

CHAPTER 6

The Marcuse-Jung Synthesis: The Feminization of Political Thought

This chapter introduces the discussion of an outgrowth of the attempted synthesis between Marcuse and Jung. The arguments presented here are not found as such in either Marcuse or Jung but are the result of interpretation and extension. "Feminization" is the term used to express the process of therapeutic reintegration of those elements which have been excluded from the dominant mode of consciousness.

Jung's process of individuation or integration begins with the conflict between what is conscious and what is unconscious. Jung represents this initial conflict as a clash between the father-spirit consciousness and the mother-moist unconscious since, for Jung, the unconscious is feminine.[1] It is possible to extend the comparison between Jung's collective unconscious and Marcuse's aesthetic dimension. For Marcuse, the aesthetic dimension, like Jung's collective unconscious, is feminine. Women, Marcuse argues, "embody" aesthetic qualities: "But beneath the social factors which determine male aggressiveness and female receptivity, a *natural* contrast exists: it is the woman who 'embodies, in a literal sense, the promise of peace, of joy, of the end of violence.[2]" He contends that the definite negation of the male principle which governs modern industrial society would be a female society, a process which, for Marcuse, involves the "femalization of the male," a reduction of the primary aggressiveness that governs patriarchal culture—in effect, a change in the instinctual structure.[3] Marcuse reasons that, since women have been less brutalized by the Per-

formance Principle, they remain closer to their sensitivity; and
his therapeutic vision is essentially a cry for the reintegration of this
feminine-aesthetic dimension.

Jung's feminine principle or anima combines the good and the
beautiful, useful and useless, morality and aesthetics.[4] This is
important for Marcuse because, as previously noted, the separation
of the useful and the beautiful led (in his theory) to a consignment
of aesthetic qualities to a separate dimension. Marcuse's vision
taps the power of the aesthetic dimension:

> True, the aesthetic dimension is a vital dimension of freedom; true, it
> repels violence, cruelty, brutality and by this token will become an essen-
> tial quality of a free society, not as a separate realm of "higher culture," but
> as a driving force and *motive* in the *construction* of such a society.[5]

For both Jung and Marcuse the therapeutic process is one of
"feminization," that is, the reactivation and reincorporation of
those elements which have been excluded from consciousness. Neumann, a Jungian scholar, offers a metaphoric explanation of this
exclusionary process. It is appropriate to turn to his comments for
an understanding of the psychological processes involved in the
formation of one-dimensional consciousness.

Newmann posits a developmental sequence for psyche and
species. In respect to ego-consciousness (following Jung closely
here), Neumann contends that ontogeny racapitulates phylogeny.
The individual and the species must pass through the same archetypal stages. Initially, there is a uroboric unity. The World Parents
are joined; there is a vision of the Great and Good Mother, of
womb safety and paradise. There is no division; existence is womb-
oneness. From the perspective of the autonomous ego, the uroboros can be seen as Eden or Engulfment, enticing or entrapping.
Uroboric incest symbolizes surrender to the mother. Consciousness
becomes conceived of as deliverance from the uroboros. The ego,
not yet autonomous, fears the supremacy of the uroboros. Suffering and death come with ego-consciousness. To leave the uroboros
is to begin to become conscious of death and the passage of time.
As Neumann notes, "Detachment from the uroboros means being
born and descending into the lower world of reality, full of dangers

and discomforts."[6] Man, in order to master the fear of engulfment by the uroboros, constructs defenses. In this, the Great Mother stage, woman is repressed. Institutions, laws, and taboos are constructed by the male collective in an attempt to break this desire to return to the uroboros, to surrender the autonomy of egoic consciousness.

Through the separation of the World Parents heaven and earth are distinguished from one another, polarity is created, and the light set free. It is a mythological representation of the ego, poised between the lower feminine world of earth and body, and the higher, masculine world of heaven and spirit. But since consciousness and the ego always experience themselves as masculine, this lower earth-world is taken to be the world of the Great Mother, and consequently hostile to the ego, while heaven is sensed as the ego-friendly world of the spirit, later personified as the All-Father.[7]

The unconscious, however, can have a positive therapeutic value through a process Jung and Neumann call "compensation," which equalizes "one-sided deviation."[8]

Neumann is concerned with the concept of the feminine in terms of its meaning and the consequences of its exclusion from and repression in Western thought. When Neumann examines the feminine, he is in fact examining an archetype, for the Great Mother is part of the Archetypal Feminine. The Feminine, for Neumann, has an elementary' and a transformative character.[9] The elementary character pertains to that aspect of the feminine that tends to surround and contain—the Feminine as Great Round, as Great Container. The clinging, swallowing elementary character is accompanied by the transformative character. The elementary character is connected to protecting, the transforming character to warmth and nurturance. Regardless of the circumstances surrounding ego development, development out of womb is regarded as rejection. Birth is genesis but also rejection. In the matriarchal stage, the transformative character is permitted its function; the archetype of the Great Mother is dominant, and the unconscious is the director. In matriarchal consciousness, the original form of consciousness, the unconscious is more spontaneous and consciousness is more receptive.[10] According to Neumann, we can still see this unconscious productivity in primitives, children, and creative individuals. Unfortunately, this healing, transformative character of the Feminine is repressed along with the elementary character. How weak are you, ego-consciousness, that you must repress to this extent that which you fear? How great is your fear and how weak is your belief in your own autonomy and strength? Sartre argues that the anti-Semite reacts to the Jew out of fear. The anti-Semite sees a Manichaean world wherein the elimination of the Jew will result in the triumph and ascendancy of the good.[11] In a similar fashion, the male egoic-consciousness sees only the elementary clinging character of the Feminine and, out of fear, represses the elementary and the transformative characters. Supposedly, autonomy for the ego will come as a result of the repression of what is non-ego; but modern man in effect has repressed what can save him:

> This patriarchal consciousness that says, "The victory of the male lies in the spiritual principle," devaluates the moon and the feminine element to which it belongs. It is "merely of the soul," "merely," the highest form of an earthly and material development that stands in opposition to the "pure spirit" that in its Apollonian-Platonic and Jewish-Christian form has led to the abstract conceptuality of modern consciousness. But this modern consciousness is threatening the existence of Western mankind, for the one-sidedness of masculine development has led to a hypertrophy of consciousness at the expense of the whole man.[12]

The consciousness which accompanies and reinforces one-dimensional society is one-sidedly masculine. All that is unknowable and dark—all that is not quantifiable and measurable—is devalued, defused, or repressed. In its place, one-dimensional society would substitute a created, perverse uroboros. This uroboric unity, as Marcuse has noted, is everywhere, and it is one-dimensional. We are offered the safety of the womb. The psyches which develop in the confines of this perverted uroboros are not autonomous.

The political, which began as a symbolic ordering of the chaos, repressed what was unconscious and feminine. It becomes the therapeutic function of political philosophy to reintegrate male and female. Marcuse speaks of the development of society from matriarchy to patriarchy. The psychic equivalent of pre-genital morality is an identification with the mother. Marcuse uses Odier's term *superid* as an alternative to the reality principle, as representative of "traces of a different, lost reality, or lost relation between ego and reality."[13] This maternal libidinal morality, Marcuse contends, would not be bound to the father but would be traceable in the instinctual structure.

> At this primary stage of the relation between "pre-ego" and reality, the Narcissistic and the maternal Eros seem to be one, and the primary experience of reality is that of a libidinous union. The Narcissistic phase of individual pre-genitality "recalls" the maternal phase of the history of the human race.[14]

The parallels between Marcuse and Neumann are evident. Marcuse, like Neumann, views the development of the species and the psyche as a process away from original unity and toward a one-sided devaluation of what is unconscious and feminine. Marcuse, like Neuman and Jung, conceives of the therapeutic function as one of reintegration of the feminine.

Plato's metaphor of the cave expresses this devaluation of the unconscious feminine. His allegory is symptomatic of subsequent developments in Western thought. Plato's dwellers are trapped in the cave-tomb-womb of the Mother. In the cave there is darkness; and what can be seen is accessible only through reflection, only through the reflection of consciousness, of the firelight. The cave is unconscious, feminine, unknowable. Plato links darkness and unknowing; however, he is aware that it is not the darkness itself that is responsible for the illusions. It is the intrusion of the firelight into the cave which destroys the darkness and substitutes shadows for darkness. The light is good, and to get to the light we have to get out of the cave. The sun is good; the sun is light, masculine, and ego-consciousness. Beware of the cave, the Great Container. If a person who has ascended into the light should attempt to re-enter the cave, he will be destroyed by those who dwell in the cave. The direction of ego development, for Plato, must be linear: no looking back, no further relationship with the cave lest you be engulfed. Never return to the cave, sun-dweller. The cave is dark and will suck you in. It will give you nothing; it will destroy you. The cave is dangerous; the unconscious feminine can be all-encompassing, destructive. The good, the true, and the beautiful come not in the combination of the cave and sun, light and darkness, but in life in the sun. With Plato, it is not tension between the poles which is important but the devaluation of one of the polarities. There is no fear of too much sun.

Admittedly, any attempt to apply this paradigm to the analysis of the tradition of political philosophy is subject to fault. At times, it too appears to approach Manichaeanism. What is interesting, however, is the almost total *exclusion* of this type of consideration from political philosophy. Marcuse is an exception. For Marcuse, the consciousness of advanced industrial society is sun-struck. His therapeutic vision would restore this tension between light and dark and would remove the devaluation of the darkness, recognizing its potential as a healing force. He would release qualities heretofore confined to the realm of higher culture for incorporation into material existence. The patriarchal culture has been governed by aggressiveness. The world and the ego, Marcuse contends, are now seen as "other." The relationship to them is one of aggressive acquisition. Any qualitative change necessitates the emergence of a "new sensibility" and a "new rationality." Aggressive acquisition must be replaced by receptivity.

In *The Great Mother*, Neumann argues that the present-day patriarchal culture suffers from a one-sided development of male intellectual consciousness. The political, as discussed by Gunnell, arise as a response to chaos. Our conception of the political, as a method of defense against engulfment by the uroboros or Great Mother, has emphasized the Father at the expense of the Mother. The therapeutic function of political philosophy must take as its task the reintegration of the Mother. In other words, the consciousness of present-day society is out of balance; it lacks a balancing dimension in the form of the archetypal world of the Feminine. To effect a cure, this is, to stand in a therapeutic relationship to this culture, is to examine and reintegrate the repressed elements of the Feminine. As Neumann notes,

Western mankind must arrive at a synthesis that includes the feminine world—which is also one-sided in its isolation. Only then will the individual human being be able to develop the psychic wholeness that is urgently needed if Western man is to face the dangers that threaten his existence from within and without.[15]

In the fourth stage of Neuman's developmental sequence, the ego reclaims that which is feminine.[16] If individuation is a search to integrate conscious and unconscious, then the individual must face the chaos before wholeness can be attained. For Marcuse, the reintegration process is dialectical: "Here too the historical process is dialectical: the patriarchal society has created a female image, a female counter-force, which may still become one of the grave-diggers of patriarchal society."[17] Symbols become the means of approach and achieve this reintegration. A symbol can make "accessible to our consciousness something that is inaccessible to our direct sensory experience and to our reason."[18]

Marcuse's symbols were powerless but not valueless. It is possible to learn from Marcuse's initial attempts. The political philosopher, to be truly creative, must employ symbols in his vision which activate the side of the feminine similar to what Ulanov calls "the divine madness of the soul described in Plato's Phaedrus, which invokes primeval forces that take us out of the limitations and conventions of social norms and the reasonable life."[19] Only then can the vision be effective and creative:

Only by relating to the reality of the soul—the freed captive—can we make the link with the unconscious truly creative, for creativity in all its forms is always the product of a meeting between the masculine world of ego consciousness and the feminine world of the soul.[20]

Modern art, as Jung sees it, does not involve this creative process but, instead, "Compensates the attitude of the conscious mind and anticipates change to come."[21] Great art, Jung argues, previously had derived its "fruitfulness" from myth and symbolization. Modern art, however, is "the symptom of a mood of world destruction and world renewal that has set its mark on our age."[22] For Jung, like Marcuse, the time is right for a metamorphosis. Jung, again like Marcuse, bases this desired metamorphosis on a reactivation of the feminine. Both Jung and Marcuse conceive of the feminine symbolically as a mode of being, as expressive of certain qualities; and it is the reintegration of these qualities which constitutes their therapeutic visions.

For Jung, to be without sexual distinction is to be without physical structure.[23] However, it is not necessary to confine the anima to men (as does Jung) when speaking symbolically. To speak of the anima is to speak of Eros as opposed to Logos. Creativity is not limited to men; the anima archetype is not a male prerogative. For Hillman, therapy becomes love of the soul. According to Hillman,

> The teaching and healing therapist—if we use the Socratic-Platonic model of philosopher who teaches and heals—is on the same plane of being as the lover; both take their origins from the same primordial impulse behind their seeking (Phaedrus, 248D).[24]

Hillman is helpful in elaborating the connections Marcuse expressed between the unconscious, the feminine, and the aesthetic. It is beauty, Hillman notes, which first draws Eros to Psyche. Beauty can be thought of not as embellishment or an avoidance but as a model for the psyche. Hillman argues:

> Perhaps we may realize that the development of the feminine, of anima into psyche, and of the soul's awakening is a process in beauty. This implies that the criteria of aesthetics—unity, line, rhythm, tension, elegance—may be transposed to the psyche, giving us a new set of qualities for appreciating what is going on in a psychological process.[25]

Images contained in the unconscious become aesthetic forms which can revitalize and beautify, the New Sensibility.

Shulamith Firestone's work in *The Dialectic of Sex* is an example of the application of this type of analysis to problems in social theory. Firestone, perhaps overly simplistically, argues that reasons of nature are no longer valid as the basis of sex distinction; she contends that humanity has gone beyond the limitations of nature—that nature is no longer valid in terms of definition in relation to the sex distinction.

Firestone, who notes the similarity between Freud and the feminist movement in their mutual treatment of the question of the subjection of women and the repression of sex, parallels Neumann's developmental sequence. In addition, her comments on culture bear a close similarity to those of Marcuse, although she does not appear to acknowledge any similarity between her formulations and those of Marcuse. The Aesthetic Mode of culture, according to Firestone, was the original method of imposing order on a mysterious and chaotic universe. Man, she contends, was able to picture but not create an ideal universe. Until the Renaissance, she hypothesizes, culture was the realm of the high priest; the Female Principle was elevated, reigning mysteriously and uncontrollably. This corresponded to the matriarchal stage of civilization. Renaissance men were men of culture in the Aesthetic Mode, man as artist, as practitioner in the realm of the Female Principle.

After the Renaissance (and this bears similarity to Marcuse's thoughts on the development of affirmative culture), aesthetic culture, according to Firestone, became reduced to what we now know as the arts and humanities. By becoming diffused, the Aesthetic Mode became weakened, the development noted by Marcuse in relation to one-dimensional society. Philosophy for Firestone defected from the classical conception; it, like pure science, left what Marcuse would call the realm of the beautiful for the realm of the useful. Art by definition, Firestone argues, had always been removed from the "real world"; however, it had always had a social function, to satisfy (artificially) wishes that reality couldn't satisfy. For Firestone, like Marcuse, the rise of the bourgeois was linked to the erosion of the aesthetic culture: "The cultural mode favored by this new, heavily patriarchal bourgeois was the 'male' Technological Mode—objective, realistic, factual, 'commonsense'—rather than the effeminate, other worldly, 'romantic idealist' Aesthetic Mode."[26]

Firestone concludes that we are now in a transitional period. This is the time in which three areas will merge: applied science, pure research, and pure modern art. This pre-revolutionary stage also foreshadows the melting together of sex categories. Firestone, unlike Jung and Marcuse, does not wish to maintain the tension between the sexes. For her, the dialectic of sex must result in some kind of synthesis, but it is doubtful whether this synthesis will retain any of the dialectical tension so important to Jung and Marcuse.

Like Marcuse, Firestone speaks of the breakdown of the realm of higher culture and its infusion as a model into the material mode of being. Her therapeutic vision, like that of Jung and Marcuse, identifies curing with regeneration. However, in addition to the question of the maintenance of tension, there are differences between Firestone and Marcuse. Her merger would "suffocate" pure high art as an offshoot of the coming together of the Technological Mode and Aesthetic Mode. For Marcuse, art will always be art. That is, it will always remain distinct from the "real," concrete world. This tension between the ideal and the actual is, for Marcuse, the essence of art. Again, it is difficult to understand whether Firestone is definitive in regard to the existence or elimination of this tension. It is possible to argue that she believes that technological advances make utopian speculation a reality. In this case, she would be close to echoing Marcuse's idea in his essay "The End of Utopia."

It was previously noted that dialectical tension is the essence of Marcuse's therapeutic vision. The attempted synthesis between Marcuse and Jung was undertaken to give Marcuse's symbols and vision an added dimension which could provide the necessary tension to withstand the diffusing capacity of one-dimensional society. It would appear, however, that the two contemporary theorists who come the closest to approximating Marcuse's therapeutic vision, Hillman and Firestone, call not for the heightening but the removal of tension. It is perhaps worthwhile to note that it is for this reason in particular that Marcuse is critical of Norman O. Brown. Marcuse believes that Brown substitutes mystical oneness for dialectical tension. For Marcuse, even unity contains this dialectical tension; harmony is never without vital tension. Firestone, as previously noted, appears to desire the elimination of tension both in regard to sex distinctions and in the relation between art and reality. As she notes, "The cultural revolution, like the economic revolution, must be predicated on the elimination of (sex) dualism at the origins not only of class, but also of cultural division."[27] Hillman appears to be closer to Firestone than Marcuse in this regard. He speaks in terms of the symbols of Western scientific tradition. For Hillman, Apollo represents "the purified objectivity and the scientific clarity of masculine consciousness."[28]

This, he contends, reflects an Apollonic fantasy of female inferiority. The reintegration of what Hillman refers to as psychological feminity becomes everyone's problem:

> The Apollonic fantasy, however, is not exclusively male, pertaining only to how men think and what they do. As an archetypal structure, it is independent of the gender of the person through whom it works, so that the integration of the feminine is a concern pertaining not only to men but to women as well. Moreoever, since the Apollonic structure is archetypal, the integration of feminity into this structure is an archetypal problem beyond the human level of personal needs and personal development. We are speaking about a kind of consciousness and the limitations imposed upon this consciousness by its archetypal structure. Our phantasies and the perceptions which they govern cannot change until this structure changes.[29]

He is arguing that we must change our conception of what it means and is to be conscious. We must develop another way of being-in the world, or this image of the inferior female and its side effects will continue to permeate our consciousness. Hillman's new consciousness would involve a taking back of the feminine of the primal union. He contends that what we have referred to previously as "consciousness" is really "the Apollonic mode as hardened by the hero into a 'strong ego' and which has predetermined the nature of the Dionysian in terms of its own bias."[30] It is Dionysius who serves as Hillman's symbol of this new consciousness. Dionysius, for Hillman, indicates an "androgynous consciousness," that is, a consciousness where the *coniunctio* is given, not attained.

Marcuse may or may not have been the "guru" of the student movement of the 1960s. It is possible, however, that one of his more significant contributions will prove to be the basis he has discovered for a "feminization" of political philosophy.

Plato used the metaphor of the philosopher as physician. The for a "feminization" of political philosophy.

Plato used the metaphor of the philosopher as physician. The metaphor of the political philosopher as therapist is an elaboration of Plato's original idea. Political philosophers, above all else, are interpreters. This metaphor allows them to interpret the political implications of discoveries in psychoanalytical thought. Moreover, the metaphor of political philosophy as therapy allows the political philosopher to focus on the diagnostic and curative elements of his task. It suggests an entire language, the language of psychoanalysis, to assist him in the conceptualization and execution of his vision of health.

The strength of Marcuse's work lies in his recognition of the therapeutic power of political philosophy. This work has attempted to bring his thought closer to the psychoanalytical thinker he personally rejects, C.G. Jung. Marcuse attempted to adapt Freud to the task of political philosophy and was subsequently forced to distort Freud's own thought. Such a distortion would not have been necessary if Marcuse had turned not to Freud but to Jung. This study has suggested a new way in which to look at Marcuse, a way which suggests both the power of his ideas and the importance of the approach itself.

NOTES

1. Jung, *Dreams*, p. 126.

2. Marcuse, *Counterrevolution and Revolt*, p. 77.

3. Ibid., p. 75.

4. Jung, *The Archetypes and the Collective Unconscious*, p. 28.

5. Marcuse, *Counterrevolution and Revolt*, p. 68.

6. Erich Neumann, *The Origins and History of Consciousness* (1949), trans. R.F.C. Hull (New York: Harper and Brothers, 1954), p. 45.

7. Ibid., p. 315.

8. Ibid., p. 330.

9. Erich Neumann, *The Great Mother*, trans. Ralph Manheim, Bollingen Series 47 (Princeton: Princeton University Press, 1963), p. 24.

10. Neumann, *Origins and History*, pp. 78-79.

11. Jean-Paul Sartre, *Anti-Semite and Jew*, trans. George J. Becker (New York: Schocken Books, 1948), pp. 40-41.

12. Neumann, *Great Mother*, p. 57.

13. Marcuse, *Eros and Civilization*, p. 209.

14. Ibid., p. 210.

15. Neumann, *Great Mother*, p. XIII.

16. Ann Belford Ulanov, *The Feminine in Jungian Psychology and in Christian Theology* (Evanston: Northwestern University Press, 1971), p. 70.

17. Marcuse, *Counterrevolution and Revolt*, p. 78.

18. Ulanov, *Feminine and Christian*, p. 21.

19. Ibid., p. 159.

20. Neumann, *Origins and History*, p. 355.

21. Jung, *Undiscovered Self*, p. 121.

22. Ibid., pp. 122-23.

23. Ulanov, *Feminine and Christian*, p. 145.

24. James Hillman, *The Myth of Analysis* (Evanston: Northwestern University Press, 1972), p. 90.

25. Ibid., pp. 101-102.

26. Shulamith Firestone, *The Dialectic of Sex* (New York: William Morrow and Company, 1970), p. 207.

27. Ibid., p. 214.

28. Hillman, *The Myth of Analysis*, p. 225.

29. Ibid., p. 250.

30. Ibid., p. 290.

A Selected Bibliography

BOOKS

Altizer, Thomas J.J. "The Religious Meaning of Myth and Symbol." In *Truth, Myth, and Symbol*, edited by Thomas J.J. Altizer, William A. Beardslee, and J. Harvey Young. Englewood Cliffs, N.J.: Prentice-Hall, Inc., 1962.

Arendt, Hannah. *The Human Condition*. Chicago: University of Chicago Press, 1958.

Bardwick, Judith M. *Psychology of Women*. New York: Harper and Row, 1971.

Bennett, E.A. *What Jung Really Said*. New York: Schocken Books, 1966.

Birnback, Martin. *Neo-Freudian Social Philosophy*. Stanford: Stanford University Press, 1961.

Breines, Paul, ed. *Critical Interruptions*. New York: Herder and Herder, Inc., 1970.

Brown, Bruce. *Marx, Freud, and the Critique of Everyday Life*. New York: Monthly Review Press, 1973.

Cassirer, Ernst. *An Essay on Man*. New Haven: Yale University Press, 1944.

Clecak, Peter. *Radical Paradoxes*. New York: Harper and Row, 1973.

Cranston, Maurice, ed. *The New Left*. New York: Library Press, 1971.

Diggins, John P. *The American Left in the Twentieth Century*. New York: Harcourt Brace Jovanovich, Inc., 1973.

Edelman, Murray. *The Symbolic Uses of Politics*. Urbana: University of Illinois Press, 1964.

———. *Politics as Symbolic Action*. Chicago: Markham Publishing Co., 1971.

Eliade, Mircea. *The Myth of the Eternal Return*. Translated by Willard Trask. Bollingen Series 46. Princeton: Princeton University Press, 1954.
———. *Myths, Dreams, and Mysteries*. Translated by Philip Mairet. New York: Harper and Row, Harper Torchbooks, 1957.
———. *The Sacred and the Profane*. Translated by Willard R. Trask. New York: Harcourt, Brace and World, Inc., Harvest Book, 1959.
———. *Images and Symbols*. Translated by Philip Mairet. New York: Sheed and Ward, 1961.
Entralgo, Pedro Lain. *The Therapy of the Word in Classical Antiquity*. Translated by L.J. Rather and John M. Sharp. New Haven: Yale University Press, 1970.
Fabry, Joseph B. *The Pursuit of Meaning*. Boston: Beacon Press, 1968.
Firestone, Shulamith. *The Dialectic of Sex*. New York: William Morrow and Company, Inc., 1970.
Frank, Jerome D. *Persuasion and Healing*. Baltimore: The Johns Hopkins Press, 1961.
Frankl, Viktor E. *The Will to Meaning*. New York: World Publishing Company, 1969.
Freud, Sigmund. *Civilization and Its Discontents* (1929). Translated and edited by James Strachey. New York: W.W. Norton and Company, Inc., 1961.
———. *The Future of An Illusion* (1927). Translated by W.D. Robson-Scott. New York: Doubleday and Company, Inc., Anchor Books, 1961.
———. *A General Introduction to Psychoanalysis* (1920). Translated by Joan Riviere. New York: Washington Square Press, Inc., 1966.
Glover, Edward. *Freud or Jung?* London: George Allen and Unwin Ltd., 1950.
Gunnell, John G. *Political Philosophy and Time*. Middletown, Conn.: Wesleyan University Press, 1968.
Hauser, Arnold. *The Philosophy of Art History*. New York: Alfred A. Knopf, 1959.
Hegel, G.W.F. *The Philosophy of History*. Translated by J. Sibree. New York: P.F. Collier and Sons, 1901.
Hillman, James. *The Myth of Analysis*. Evanston: Northwestern University Press, 1972.
Horowitz, Gad. *Repression*. Toronto: University of Toronto Press, 1977.
Howe, Irving, ed. *Beyond the New Left*. New York: McCall Publishing Company, 1970.
Jacobi, Jolande. *Complex/Archetype/Symbol*. Translated by Ralph Manheim. New York: Pantheon Books, Inc., 1959.
James, Elizabeth M. *Political Theory: An Introduction to Interpretation*. Chicago: Rand McNally College Publishing Company, 1976.

Jay, Martin. *The Dialectical Imagination*. Boston: Little, Brown and Company, 1973.

Jung, Carl G. *Collected Papers on Analytical Psychology*. London: Bailliere, Tindall and Cox, 1922.

―――. *Psychology of the Unconscious*. London: Kegan Paul, Trench, Trubner and Co. Ltd., 1922.

―――. *Psychological Types*. Translated by H. Godwin Baynes. New York: Harcourt, Brace and Company, Inc., 1926.

―――. *Modern Man in Search of a Soul*. London: Kegan Paul, Trench, Trubner and Co. Ltd., 1933.

―――. *Two Essays on Analytical Psychology*. Translated by R.F.C. Hull. Bollingen Series 20 Vol. 7. Princeton: Princeton University Press, 1953.

―――. *The Practice of Psychotherapy*. Translated by R.F.C. Hull. Bollingen Series 20, Vol. 16. New York: Pantheon Books, 1954.

―――. *Symbols of Transformation*. Translated by R.F.C. Hull. Bollingen Series 20. Vol 5. Princeton: Princeton University Press, 1956.

―――. *The Undiscovered Self*. Translated by R.F.C. Hull. New York: Mentor Books, 1957.

―――. *The Archetypes and the Collective Unconscious*. Translated by R.F.C. Hull. Bollingen Series 20. Princeton: Princeton University Press, 1974.

―――. *Dreams*. Translated by R.F.C. Hull. Bollingen Series 20. Princeton: Princeton University Press, 1974.

Kafka, Franz. *The Trial*. Translated by Willa Muir and Edwin Muir. New York: Schocken Books, 1968.

Kaplan, Abraham. "Freud and Modern Philosophy." In *Freud and the Twentieth Century*, edited by Benjamin Nelson. London: George Allen and Unwin Ltd., 1958.

Kauffman, Walter. *Nietzsche*. New York: Vintage Books, 1968.

King, Richard. *The Party of Eros*. Chapel Hill: University of North Carolina Press, 1972.

Laing, R.D. *The Politics of Experience*. New York: Ballantine Books, 1967.

Langer, Susanne K. *Philosophy in a New Key* (1942). Cambridge, Mass.: Harvard University Press, 1963.

Lipshires, Sidney. *Herbert Marcuse: From Marx to Freud and Beyond*. Cambridge, Mass.: Schenkman Publishing Company, 1974.

MacIntyre, Alasdair. *Herbert Marcuse: An Exposition and a Polemic*. New York: Viking Press, 1970.

Marcuse, Herbert. "The Foundation of Historical Materialism (1932)." In *Studies in Critical Philosophy*, translated by Javis De Bres. Boston: Beacon Press, 1972.

―――. "Affirmative Character of Culture (1937)." In *Negations*, translated by Jeremy J. Shapiro. Boston: Beacon Press, 1968.

———. "Aggressiveness in Advanced Industrial Society" (no date given). In *Negations*, translated by Jeremy J. Shapiro. Boston: Beacon Press, 1968.

———. "Philosophy and Critical Theory (1937)." In *Negations*, translated by Jeremy J. Shapiro. Boston: Beacon Press, 1968.

———. *Reason and Revolution (1941)*. (Boston: Beacon Press, 1960.

———. "Sartre's Existentialism (1948)." In *Studies in Critical Philosophy*, translated by Javis De Bres. Boston: Beacon Press, 1972.

———. *Eros and Civilization*. New York: Random House, 1955.

———. *Soviet Marxism: A Critical Analysis*. New York: Columbia University Press, 1958.

———. "Obsolescence of the Freudian Concept of Man (1963)." In *Five Lectures*. Boston: Beacon Press, 1970.

———. *One-Dimensional Man*. Boston: Beacon Press, 1964.

———. "Repressive Tolerance." In *A Critique of Pure Tolerance*, edited by Robert Paul Wolff, Barrington Moore, Jr., and Herbert Marcuse. Boston: Beacon Press, 1965.

———. "The End of Utopia (1967)," In *Five Lectures*. Boston: Beacon Press, 1970.

———. "Love Mystified: A Critique of Norman O. Brown (1967)," In *Negations*, translated by Jeremy J. Shapiro. Boston: Beacon Press, 1968.

———. "Progress and Freud's Theory of Instincts (1968)." In *Five Lectures*. Boston: Beacon Press, 1970.

———. *An Essay on Liberation*. Boston: Beacon Press, 1969.

———. "Art as a Form of Reality." In *On the Future of Art*. Sponsored by the Solomon R. Guggenheim Museum. New York: Viking Press, 1970.

———. *Counterrevolution and Revolt*. Boston: Beacon Press, 1972.

Marks, Robert W. *The Meaning of Marcuse*. New York: Ballantine Books, 1970.

Marx, Karl. *A Contribution to the Critique of Political Economy*. Translated by S.W. Ryazanskaya. Edited by Maurice Dobb. New York: International Publishers, New World Paperbacks, 1970.

Neumann, Erich. *The Origins and History of Consciousness* (1949). Translated by R.F.C. Hull. New York: Harper and Brothers, 1954.

———. *The Great Mother*. Translated by Ralph Manheim. Bollingen Series 47. Princeton: Princeton University Press, 1963.

Nietzsche, Friedrich. *The Birth of Tragedy* (1872). Translated by Walter Kaufmann. New York: Vintage Books, 1967.

———. *Ecce Homo* (1908). Translated by Anthony M. Ludovici. Edited by Oscar Levy. New York: Russell and Russell, Inc., 1964.

———. *Philosophy in the Tragic Age of the Greeks*. Translated by Marianne Cowan. Chicago: Henry Regnery Company, Gateway Edition, 1962.

Philipson, Morris. *An Outline of a Jungian Aesthetics*. Evanston: Northwestern University Press, 1963.

Progoff, Ira. *Jung's Psychology and Its Social Meaning*. New York: Julian Press, Inc. 1953.

Robinson, Paul A. *The Freudian Left*. New York: Harper and Row, 1969.

Roszak, Theodore. *The Making of a Counter Culture*. Garden City, N.Y.: Doubleday and Company, Inc. 1969.

Sartre, Jean-Paul. *Anti-Semite and Jew*. Translated by George J. Becker. New York: Schocken Books, 1948.

Schiller, Friedrich. *On the Aesthetic Education of Man—In a Series of Letters* (1795). Edited and translated by Elizabeth M. Wilkinson and L.A. Willoughby. Oxford: Clarendon Press, 1967.

Sebba, Gregor. "Truth and Myth in Modern Rationalistic Societies." In *Truth, Myth, and Symbol*, edited by Thomas J.J. Altizer, William A. Beardslee, and J. Harvey Young. Englewood Cliffs, N.J.: Prentice-Hall, Inc. 1962.

Spector, Jack J. *The Aesthetics of Freud*. New York: Praeger Publishers, 1972.

Spragens, Thomas A., Jr. *Understanding Political Theory*. New York: St. Martin's Press, 1976.

Tudor, Henry. *Political Myth*. New York: Praeger Publishers, 1972.

Ulanov, Ann Belford. *The Feminine in Jungian Psychology and in Christian Theology*. Evanston: Northwestern University Press, 1971.

Vivas, Eliseo. *Contra Marcuse*. New York: Dell Publishing Co., 1971.

Weber, Shierry M. "Individuation as Praxis." In *Critical Interruptions*, edited by Paul Breines. New York: Herder and Herder, Inc., 1970.

Wind, Edgar. *Art and Anarchy*. New York: Random House, 1969.

Woddis, Jack. *New Theories of Revolution*. New York: International Publishers, 1972.

Wolff, Kurt H., and Moore, Barrington, Jr., eds. *The Critical Spirit*. Boston: Beacon Press, 1967.

Wolin, Sheldon S. *Politics and Vision*. Boston: Little, Brown and Company, 1960.

ARTICLES

Abel, L. "Seven Heroes of the New Left." *New York Times Magazine*, May 5, 1968, pp. 30-31.

Andrew E. "Work and Freedom in Marcuse and Marx." *Canadian Journal of Political Science* 3 (June 1970), pp. 241-56.

Berki, R.N. "Marcuse and the Crisis of the New Radicalism: From Politics to Religion?." *Journal of Politics* 34 (February 1972), pp. 56-92.

Bookman, John T. "The Disjunction of Political Science and Political Philosophy." *American Journal of Economics and Sociology* 29 (January 1970), pp. 17-24.

Braybrooke, D. "The Expanding Universe of Political Philosophy." *Review of Metaphysics* 11 (June 1958), pp. 648-72.

―――. "Marcuse's Merits." *Trans-Action* (October 1969), pp. 51-54.

Burnham, J. "Sock It to Us, Herbert." *National Review*, November 19, 1968, p. 1158.

Callahan, D. "Resistance and Technology." *Commonweal*, February 9, 1968, p. 551 f.

"Camus and Some Others." *Times Literary Supplement*, January 29, 1970, pp. 97-98.

Capouya, E. "What We Don't Know Might Kill Us." *Saturday Review*, March 28, 1964, pp. 26-27.

Clecak, P. "Marcuse: Ferment of Hope. *Nation*, June 16, 1969, pp. 765-68.

Clegg, Jerry S. "Freud and the 'Homeric' Mind." *Inquiry* 17 (Winter 1974), pp. 445-56.

Cobban, Alfred. "The Decline of Political Theory." *Political Science Quarterly* 68 (September 1953), pp. 321-37.

Cohen, M. "Norman Vincent Peale of the Left." *Atlantic* (June 1969), pp. 108-10.

Delany, P. "Marcuse in the Seventies." *Partisan Review*, no. 3 (1973), pp. 455-60.

Deutsch, Karl W. "On Political Theory and Political Action." *American Political Science Review* 65 (March 1971), pp. 11-27.

Edel, Abraham, "Instead of Repression." Review of *Eros and Civilization*, by Herbert Marcuse. *Nation*, July 7, 1956, p. 22.

Eidelberg, Paul. "The Temptation of Herbert Marcuse." *Review of Politics* 31 (October 1969), pp. 442-58.

Ferkiss, Victor C. "Man's Tools and Man's Choices: The Confrontation of Technology and Political Science." *American Political Science Review*, 67 (September 1973), pp. 972-80.

Fingarette, H. Review of *Eros and Civilization*, by Herbert Marcuse. *Review of Metaphysics* 10 (June 1957), pp. 660-65.

Fordham, Michael. "Reflections on Image and Symbol." *Journal of Analytical Psychology* 2 (January 1957), pp. 85-92.

Fremstad, John. "Marcuse: The Dialectics of Hopelessness." *Western Political Quarterly* 30 (March 1977), pp. 80-92.

Frohock, Fred M. "Notes on the Concept of Politics." *Journal of Politics* 36 (May 1974), pp. 379-408.

Girgus, Sam B. "Howells and Marcuse: A Forecast of the One-Dimensional Age." *American Quarterly* 25 (March 1973), pp. 108-18.

Glaser, K. "Marcuse and the German New Left." *National Review*, July 2, 1968, p. 649 f.

Glass, James M. "Plato, Marx, and Freud: Therapy, Eros, and the Rampage of Thanatos." Paper delivered at the meeting of the Southern Political Science Association, Atlanta, Ga., November 1972.

———. "The Yogin and the Utopian: Nirvana and the Discovery of Being." *Polity* 5 (Summer 1973), pp. 428-50.

———. "The Philosopher and the Shaman: The Political Vision as Incantation." *Political Theory* 2 (May 1974), pp. 181-96.

———. "Machiavelli's Prince and Alchemical Transformation: Action and the Archetype of Regeneration." *Polity* 8 (Summer 1976), pp. 503-28.

———. "Political Philosophy as Therapy: Rousseau and the Pre-Social Origins of Consciousness." *Political Theory* 4 (May 1976), pp. 163-84.

Gold, H. "California Left: Mao, Marx, et Marcuse." *Saturday Evening Post*, October 19, 1968, pp. 56-59.

Goldman, Lucien. "Understanding Marcuse." *Partisan Review*, no. 3 (1971), pp. 247-62.

Goodwin, R. "Social Theory of Herbert Marcuse." *Atlantic* (June 1971), pp. 68-70s f.

Greeman, Richard. "A Critical Re-Examination of Herbert Marcuse's Works." *New Politics* (Fall 1967).

Groutt, J. "Marcuse and Goodwin Tangle at Temple." *Commonweal*, May 23, 1969, pp. 279-80.

Hindery, R. "Marcuse's Eroticized Man." *Christian Century*, Feburary 4, 1970, pp. 136-38.

Howe, I. "Herbert Marcuse or Milovan Djilas." Review of *Eros and Civilization*, by Herbert Marcuse. *Harper's* (July 1969), p. 84f.

Jaffa, Harry B. "The Case Against Political Theory." *Journal of Politics* 22 (May 1960), pp. 259-75.

Jones, Ernest. "The Theory of Symbolism." Amplified from a paper read before the British Psychological Society, January 29, 1916. Published in *British Journal of Psychology* 9; included in *Papers on Psychoanalysis*, London: Bailliere, Tindall and Cox, 1948.

Kateb, G. "Political Thought of Herbert Marcuse." *Commentary* (January 1970), pp. 48-63.

Kress, Paul. "Self, System, and Significance: Reflections on Professor Easton's Political Science." *Ethics* 77 (October 1966), pp. 1-13.

Krieger, R.A. "Latest Dispatch from the Barricades." Review of *Counter-revolution and Revolt*, by Herbert Marcuse, *Business Week*, June 17, 1972, p. 12.

Kristol, I. "Improbable Guru of Surrealistic Politics." *Fortune* (July 1969), p. 191s f.

Landau, Martin. "On the Use of Metaphor in Political Analysis." *Social Research* 28 (Autumn 1961), pp. 331-52.

"Legion vs. Marcuse." *Nation*, October 28, 1968, p. 421.

Leiss, W. "Reply with Rejoinder to E. Andrew." *Canadian Journal of Political Science* 4 (September 1971), pp. 398-404.

McDonald, Lee C. "Myth, Politics, and Political Science." *Western Political Quarterly* 22 (March 1969), pp. 141-50.

Marcuse, Herbert. "Theory and Therapy in Freud." *Nation*, September 28, 1957, pp. 200-202.

―――. "Notes on the Problem of Historical Laws." *Partisan Review* (Winter 1959), pp. 117-29.

―――. "World Without a Logos." *Bulletin of the Atomic Scientists* 20 (January 1964), pp. 25-26.

―――. "Remarks on a Redefinition of Culture." *Daedalus* (Winter 1965), pp. 190-207.

―――. "Love Mystified: A Critique of Norman O. Brown." *Commentary* (February 1967), pp. 71-75.

―――. "Marcuse Defines His New Left Line: An Interview edited by J.L. Ferrier and others." Translated by H. Weaver. *New York Times Magazine*, October 27, 1968, pp. 29-31.

―――. "Student Protest Is Nonviolent Next to the Society Itself." *New York Times Magazine*, May 4, 1969, p. 137.

―――. "End of Utopia." *Ramparts Magazine* (April 1970), pp. 28-34.

―――. "Dear Angela." *Ramparts Magazine* (February 1971), p. 22.

―――. "A Reply to Lucien Goldman." *Partisan Review* (Winter 1971-72), pp. 397-400.

―――. "Art and Revolution." *Partisan Review* (Spring 1972), pp. 174-87.

―――. "Can Communism Be Liberal?" *New Statesman*, June 23, 1972, pp. 860-61.

―――. "When Law and Morality Stand in the Way." *Society* (September 1973), pp. 23-24.

Mark, Max. "What Image of Man for Political Science." *Western Political Quarterly* 15 (December 1962), pp. 593-604.

Minogue, K.R. "Epiphenomenalism in Politics: The Quest for Political Reality." *Political Studies* 20 (December 1972), pp. 462-74.

Montgomery, J.W. "Marcuse." *Christianity Today*, April 24, 1970, p. 47.

Odajnyk, Walter. "The Political Ideas of C.G. Jung." *American Political Science Review* 67 (March 1973), pp. 142-52.

"One-Dimensional Philosopher." *Time*, March 22, 1968, p. 38f.

Parekh, B. "Utopianism and Manicheism: A Critique of Marcuse's Theory of Revolution." *Social Research* 39 (Winter 1972), pp. 622-51.

Peretz. M. "Herbert Marcuse: Beyond Technological Reason." *Yale Review* 57 (June 1968), pp. 518-27.

Schoolman, M. "Further Reflections on Work, Alienation, and Freedom in Marcuse and Marx." *Canadian Journal of Political Science* 6 (June 1973), pp. 295-302.

Skinner, Quentin. "Meaning and Understanding in the History of Ideas." *History and Theory* 8 (November 1969), pp. 3-53.

Slater, Ian. "Orwell, Marcuse, and the Language of Politics." *Political Studies* 23 (December 1975), pp. 459-74.

Smith, Roger, "Redemption and Politics." *Political Science Quarterly* 86 (June 1971), pp. 205-31.

Sobran, M.J. "Future Future of Marcuse." *National Review* 24, December 8, 1972), p. 1352.

"Soviet Marxism: A Critical Analysis." Review of *Soviet Marxism*, by Herbert Marcuse. *Review of Political Studies* 7 (June 1959), pp. 181-83.

Sparrow, J. "Marcuse: The Gospel of Hate." Review of *An Essay on Liberation*, by Herbert Marcuse. *National Review*, October 21, 1969, pp. 1068-69.

Spitz, David. "Pure Tolerance." *Dissent* (September-October 1966), pp. 510-25.

Stein, Leopold. "What Is a Symbol Supposed to Be?" *Journal of Analytical Psychology* 2 (January 1957), pp. 73-84.

Stern, S. "Metaphysics of Rebellion." *Ramparts Magazine*, June 29, 1968, pp. 55-60.

Stillman, E. "Marcuse." *Horizon* (Summer 1969), pp. 26-31.

Sullivan, D. "Reply with Rejoinder to Callahan." *Commonweal*, February 9, 1968, p. 551sf.

Vivas, E. "Incoherent Nihilist." *National Review*, July 14, 1970, p. 739f.

Walsh, J.K. "Why Marcuse Matters." *Commonweal*, October 2, 1970, pp. 21-25.

Walton, P. "From Surplus Value to Surplus Theories: Marx, Marcuse, and MacIntyre." *Social Research* 37 (December 1970), pp. 644-55.

Walzer, Michael. "On the Role of Symbolism in Political Thought." *Political Science Quarterly* 82 (June 1967), pp. 191-204.

Wiatr, Jerzy J. "Herbert Marcuse: Philosopher of a Lost Radicalism." Translated by H.F. Mins. *Science and Society* 34 (Fall 1970), pp. 319-30.

Widmer, K. "Society as a Work of Art." Review of *Five Lectures*, by Herbert Marcuse, and *Herbert Marcuse: An Exposition and Polemic*, by Alasdair MacIntyre. *Nation*, July 6, 1970, pp. 211-23f.

Wilden, Anthony. "Marcuse and the Freudian Model: Energy, Information, and Phantasie." *Salmagundi* (Fall 1969-Winter 1970), pp. 196-245.

Wolff, Kurt H. Review of *Eros and Civilization*, by Herbert Marcuse. *American Journal of Sociology* 62 (November 1956), pp. 342-43.

Zamoshkin, I.A. and Motroshilova, N.V. "Is Marcuse's Critical Theory of Society Critical?" *Soviet Review* 11 (Spring 1970), pp. 3-24.

Zashin, Elliot, and Chapman, Phillip C. "The Uses of Metaphor and Analogy: Toward a Renewal of Political Language." *Journal of Politics* 36 (May 1974), pp. 290-326.

Zhukov, Y. "Taking Marcuse to the Woodshed." *Atlas* (September 1968), pp. 33-35.

Index

ABOUT THE AUTHOR

Gertrude A. Steuernagel teaches in the Political Science department at Kent State University, Kent, Ohio. She has published in *Polity* and is currently working on comparisons of Jung and Rousseau and Arendt and Lippmann.